69.50

69.50

DESIGNING THE
NEW LANDSCAPE

DESIGNING THE
NEW

Foreword by

GEOFFREY JELLICOE

WITH 291 ILLUSTRATIONS AND PLANS, 106 IN COLOUR

THAMES AND HUDSON

SUTHERLAND LYALL

LANDSCAPE

For Hal and Etta Proshansky

© 1991 *Thames and Hudson Ltd, London*

Printed and bound in Singapore

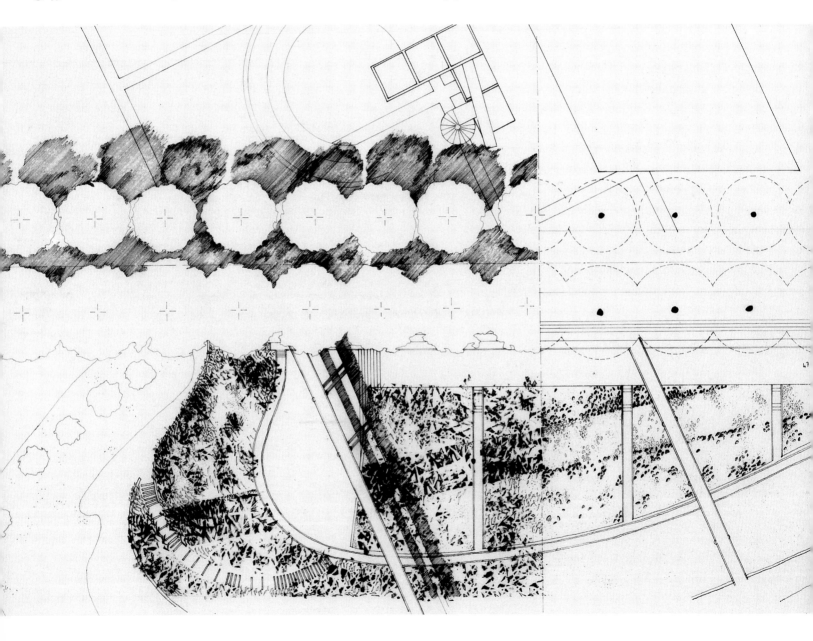

CONTENTS

FOREWORD

This book is of unusual significance to the present and future of landscape design. The examples, chosen with knowledgeable discrimination, are suggestive of a global art that has been quietly maturing over the past few years and is now breaking into flower.

In order to appreciate the importance of it in the context of history, let us enlarge upon the author's own introduction. Until about 1830 landscape design was a stylized and universal expression of the aristocrat, far removed from that first uprising of the individual in Mannerist Italy around 1600. The emergence of a thinking middle class in England was accompanied by an individual urge for a free choice of any style to which he (and now she) felt drawn – global, historic, natural, indeed anything but modern. By the end of the century the gifted laymen of all classes (with exceptions) were dominating garden design, whether of horticulture or a grand Victorian park. Then a cantankerous child was born, imprudently christened Constructivism, later to beget such movements as the International Style, Functionalism and Modernism.

It is common knowledge that the leader and inspirer of this environmental revolution was the Swiss Le Corbusier. He was a geometrician in search of what he conceived to be the truth, and nothing but the truth. His concept basically was that of the separation of cosmic structures from planet earth (illustrated by static architecture floating on pilotis above a flowing natural landscape), but he seemed impervious to the real significance of nature in human life. He dealt in universals. Nevertheless Constructivism as an art form that represented a brave new world had come to stay, surviving the most adverse conditions.

In the beginning there was no qualified landscape profession in Europe to counterbalance this determined geometry. That was to come. Two pointers in the mid-1930s were Christopher Tunnard's *Gardens in the Modern Landscape*, a voice crying in the wilderness, and Berthold Lubetkin's white flats of Highpoint, Highgate, with charming gardens and links with the woods of far-off historic Kenwood.

Now what exactly *is* Constructivism?

Curiously enough it is both geometrical *and* biological, most clearly identified by Naum Gabo and Henry Moore respectively in the 1930s publication *Circle*. It is quite simply that for the first time in the history of art the mind was directed to the structure of the whole rather than only to the exterior appearance. Moore himself insisted that it was the escape and expression of the spirit of the interior that distorted his sculpture, and that he repudiated surface beauty absolutely.

The International Style was inhuman but distinguished; not so the awful Functionalism. The scientific expression of engineering may be beautiful, but an architecture that expresses its use literally and without poetry is dead. In either case the common man felt excluded.

World War II almost destroyed the purity of the concept of Constructivism, but beneath the surface a movement was striving to counterbalance the theory of geometry (symbolized by Mondrian) with that of the biology of landscape (symbolized, oddly enough, by Picasso). It was being revealed that the arts of landscape were in fact far wider and deeper that those of architecture in their expression of the wondrous human psyche. The landscape professions increased throughout the world, and then there began to emerge the pluralism, variety and richness of idea that inform this book.

Although the examples are chosen from all parts of the world, are technically well-composed and seductive in the endless way we all know and are infinite in variety, yet there is one fundamental characteristic common to all: *the imaginative landscape extends far beyond what the eye sees and the body enjoys*; further indeed than Constructivism in its prime.

Capability Brown was the first to exploit space and time in landscape design by allowing the eye to be led direct over green hills to the sky and infinity, and the mind to wander back in time through the vehicles of mythical sculpture and architectural follies. What is happening now is a vast extension of this pioneer work; today the designs are for a multitude of minds, including those of women and children. Such gardens as that of Hamilton Finlay in Scotland with its mythological clues, or those that recall memories of childhood or foreign travel, are personal to the individual. So, too, are the abstracts such as those of Richard Long, which are meaningful only to the initiated. The really significant landscapes of present and future are without question the collective. The great national garden festivals offer a chance for the invisible to be wrapped up within the fun and games. The sponsored project will increase with prosperity: the cry that good landscape is good business is assuredly proved by Martha Schwartz's lovely frogs within a shopping centre, unquestionably lifting the spirit and encouraging the urge to buy. Above all others is the civic park with its potential power to calm, refresh, satisfy and inspire the soul of Everyman in the tradition of church and temple.

The subject of global landscape being so much more complicated than that of architecture, the author has marshalled his eclectic material in such a way that the reader is not overwhelmed by the sheer velocity of ideas. His rational approach organizes the irrational without destroying it. This well-researched, well-written and well-illustrated book invites one to pass through the time-and-space door and take a glance at what lies within and beyond.

Assuming (as one must) that our planet will not be disrupted whether by itself or, more likely, by the human species, then the potential future of landscape design throughout the world is breathtaking. Consider the millions of individuals only beginning to realize what it means to mingle on equal terms with the nature that they love but which the mind has outgrown. No wonder that landscape design may well become total, and may soon supersede architecture as the mother of the arts.

Reader, pause: and then proceed.

Geoffrey Jellicoe

INTRODUCTION

The new landscape of the last two decades is not so much a unified movement as a reassertion of landscape design's place near the centre of design and design thinking. For much of the twentieth century it had been viewed as a peripheral activity by the radical branch of architecture, that sister discipline with which historically it has been tied. Modern Movement architects have never really been comfortable with landscape. Their central preoccupations were with such things as progress, geometry, technology, order and the machine image. Landscape's organic character was inherently difficult to incorporate into that frame of reference. There was no landscape school at the pioneering Bauhaus and the landscape elements of canonical Modernist architectural designs have rarely been more than a generalized indication of natural planting. Indeed, landscape designers themselves offered no convincing Modernist schema for landscape. Their practice was anyway too intimately associated with the architecture of the previous century against which the Modernists had so radically reacted.

That has been the case until recently. Yet over the last twenty years Modernism has largely evaporated as a reigning aesthetic among architects and designers. A minor consequence of that is that many of the difficulties architects have experienced in coping with landscape have fallen away. More importantly, this development has brought a new, relaxed approach to design. In the Post-Modern era such things as eclecticism, fragmentation, layering of unrelated ordering systems, historicism, irony, metaphor and wit are all permissible. In this new aesthetic environment landscape designers have a new self-confidence. They have begun to develop radical positions which may or may not necessarily have very much to do with prevailing architectural stances and which in some cases claim aesthetic high ground over architectural design. It needs to be said that a concomitant of that has been the emergence of landscape designers formally trained in other disciplines such as painting, sculpture, architecture and environmental art. The new landscape is pluralist, drawing from a great diversity of sources and disciplines.

That has not occurred without considerable groundwork in the postwar Modernist environment by such seminal designers as Roberto Burle Marx, Thomas Church, Sylvia Crowe, Ernst Cramer and Luis Barragán, who have provided memorable visual models. And there have been others, mostly American, such as Garrett Eckbo, Ian McHarg, Lawrence Halprin, Kevin Lynch and Donald Appleyard, who have provided theoretical, perceptual and ecological frameworks for the design of landscape.

Roberto Burle Marx's Kronforth Garden, Rio de Janeiro, effectively abstract painting with plants at a vast scale.

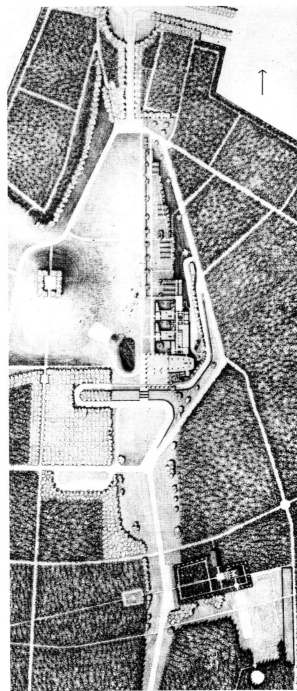

(*Left and far left*) Sigurd Lewerentz and Gunnar Asplund's Woodland Cemetery at Stockholm: canonical landscape design in which ascetic architecture and ascetic landscape are set in a forest.

The heroes

The Brazilian landscape designer Roberto Burle Marx created brightly coloured planting schemes which were in a sense large-scale abstract paintings in plant material, thus giving a new twist to the Western preoccupation with the painterly landscapes of the eighteenth and nineteenth centuries. Luis Barragán, claimed simultaneously by landscape designers and architects as their own, introduced the possibilities of the architectonic landscape with plant material featured either as background to his De Stijl-like planes of paving, coloured concrete and water or as quasi-sculptural features in a three-dimensional diagram.

In Switzerland Ernst Cramer's 1959 Poet's Garden with its lawn pyramids and abstract three-dimensional geometric forms in an underlying complexity of spatial relationships pioneered land art and helped to undermine the received view of landscape as an orthodox re-enactment of nature.

There have been some influential Modernist landscapes. Sigurd Lewerentz and Gunnar Asplund's design at the Woodland Cemetery, Stockholm,

established a relationship between ascetic architecture and an ascetic landscape of turfed undulations. In the United States Thomas Church's landscapes, small-scale, asymmetrical and in a Modernist geometrical style, complemented the Modernist houses which they surrounded, while in England Geoffrey Jellicoe's sparse and geometric landscapes sympathetically served the same function. Perhaps more relevant for the contemporary scene was Le Corbusier's scheme for Chandigarh, in which three or four different functional plans – for housing layout, motor traffic, pedestrians and landscape – were laid in careful registration over each other in a way which integrated the elements of the city plan.

In the 1960s, mainly in the United States, a group of designers and theoreticians began to investigate landscape as a participatory activity. Donald Appleyard, for example, in his *View from the Road* wrote about the experience of perceiving and moving through landscape. Lawrence Halprin explored the emotional and perceptual experience of sequential landscape. Garrett Eckbo raised the importance of the element of time, a dimension which affects this more than any other man-made environment. In *Landscape for Living* he argued that the crucial question of the quality of landscape resulted from relationships between its elements rather than from the landscape itself. It was a total involvement of the

(*Above left*) A Thomas Church domestic landscape of 1948 which combines contemporary architectural forms and geometry with natural planting.

(*Above*) A Los Angeles garden by Eckbo Dean Austin and Williams.

(*Above*) Lawrence Halprin's Lovejoy Fountain Plaza in Portland, Oregon, 1966. Ostensibly an almost schematic reduction of the underlying topography into precise contours, its use of noisy water combines to create an experience rather than a more visual stimulation.

(*Right*) Plan of Chandigarh: an overlayering of different systems forming an integrated townscape whole.

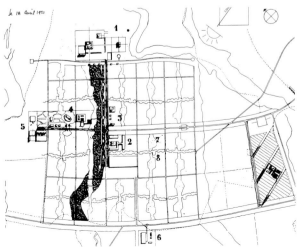

senses, more to do with the way in which people perceived the landscape than what it actually looked like. 'Our whole sense of aesthetics comes from nature, not on a picturesque level but on a biological level . . . how it interacts with [our responses]'.

These were to a large extent analyses rather than prescriptions, but they added much-needed substance to the body of theory which landscape design had otherwise failed to develop for nearly half a century.

The ecological ethic

Throughout the 1970s at the University of Pennsylvania the landscape professor Ian McHarg discussed with students (and enormous television audiences) the idea of landscape as an ecological system in which geology, topography, the disposition of aquifers, land use, vegetation, wildlife and climate were all critical elements. His scope was across the entire field of large-scale landscape and environmental planning, but there were important messages for landscapes of practically any size: he brought into focus the idea of landscape as something considerably more than a collection of artistically arranged planting and topography. What he had done was to introduce the notion of environmental ethics.

As was the case with a number of the new social sciences anxious to establish their credibility, McHarg's subtext was that landscape is something akin to a science, susceptible to the kinds of objective analysis and synthesis which characterize hard-edged academic disciplines. Behind this his implied Utilitarian (and Modernist) message was that if a landscape works as an ecological system it necessarily works as an aesthetic system.

For recent landscape designers neither proposition necessarily made sense. They have been inclined to charge the Penn School with analysing a great deal, building little and discounting formal design. As the

A summary survey map of water and land features around Philadelphia, from McHarg's *Design with Nature* of 1971.

American landscape architect David Tomlinson put it, in the magazine of the US Landscape Institute: 'Most landscape architects have failed miserably to make an original contribution to the aesthetics of the twentieth century. . . Teaching of pure design is no longer fashionable. It is far easier to teach the jargon and functionalism of modern landscape or recreational planning than to teach the aesthetic principles of pure design.' Equally questionable for the avant-garde was the Penn School's implied assumption that nature itself was the only possible model for landscape design. In the new era of pluralism that was an assumption which nobody could make any more.

Yet, at a time when the environment is at a critically fragile stage, McHarg's broad message has made an inescapable imprint on the underlying structure of landscape designers' thinking. It is an indication of the thrall of Modernism that landscape designers needed to be reminded that theirs of all crafts was inherently tied into the global ecosystem.

Japan

From the 1950s onwards another style and approach to landscape had begun to be seen as a sympathetic model: that of Japan. Its raked sand gardens with their precisely placed rocks, plants and orthogonal architectural setting seemed to belong to the spirit of Western Modernism. Here was a tradition whose Zen understatement, its rigorous, relentless reductiveness, apparently offered cultural confirmation of the predestined nature of Modernism – and also the possibility of a useful visual counterpoint to the latter's severe ethic and aesthetic.

The fact that these rock gardens were specialized, enclosed gardens for meditation, intended to be contemplated in a way and for lengths of time which no Western landscape tourist could entirely grasp, was neither here nor there. Nor was the fact that their design sprang from a completely different cultural, religious and artistic milieu. They were, even in the black and white photographs of the early 1950s, simply stunningly serene abstractions, models calling out for imitation.

If Western landscape architects, anxious to assimilate and redeploy the lessons of Japan, had to do so outside its original cultural and mystical background and with settings which were inevitably different, they were at least able to utilize some of the detail and something of its reductivist approach to design. The Japanese garden – and, as it became more widely published and seen, the larger-scale landscape – almost always used found elements such as rock, sand, pine-needles, timber and the like, placed in subtle relationships with each other. These were natural materials but they were deliberately dislocated from their original 'natural' context, brought together into visual ensembles which had new meanings in their new contexts.

Many of these materials were hard: rock, dressed stone pebbles, gravel, sand. Many Japanese gardens such as that at Ryoan-ji were devoid of soft plant

material. Yet the only word possible to describe such arrangements was 'garden'. This implicitly raised yet again the problem of the relationship between landscape and nature. As it turned out, the superficial result was the ready acceptance in the West of the notion of *hard* landscape – a term which before the war would have been considered oxymoronic by most designers.

The fifteenth-century Zen garden at Ryoan-ji, Kyoto: extreme understatement with subtle placement of the elements in their raked gravel setting.

Traditional European landscape assumptions and the problem of nature

By the mid-1970s the academic study of the history of landscape achieved a kind of critical mass. What had been a trickle of texts, with teaching, largely anecdotal, recounting visits to landscapes abroad, became the carefully researched revelation of the detail, underlying assumptions, form and meaning of the European and American tradition and, increasingly, the landscape of Islam and the East.

That was important in establishing credibility and raising the self-esteem of the landscape profession. And in the new Post-Modern era which was comfortable with eclecticism and historicism it provided designers with an increasingly rich field of sources and theory. Modernism had excluded and prohibited. Now it was possible to re-examine and experiment with attitudes, forms, details and assumptions from the whole gamut of landscape design.

With a few exceptions postwar designers had tacitly assumed that landscape was broadly about recreating nature. This was the heritage of the English garden tradition, essentially a continuation of the late-eighteenth-century Picturesque theory of the designer Humphry Repton and the writers Richard Payne Knight and Uvedale Price. Picturesque theory and practice had been modified over the next century by landscape designers such as Paxton, who translated Repton's vision into the public realm, by Alphand with the dramatic topo-graphy and planting of his Paris parks and contemporaneously in the United States by Calvert Vaux and Frederick Law Olmsted with their great public landscapes. William Robinson's concept of the wild garden in England was to be influential, at the turn of the century and on a smaller scale, on Gertrude Jekyll.

The central Picturesque tenet was that nature was the ultimate model. But nature was not always perfect in its designing. So the landscape designer's task, ran Picturesque theory, was to re-compose nature with a better design than nature was sometimes able to create. It represented a sharp reaction to the geometric order of the French and Italian landscape of earlier centuries, and also to the semi-natural serpentine curves and clumps of Capability Brown during the previous decades in England. Its visual models were admired pastoral paintings of the seventeenth century by Claude and Poussin, and the more rugged landscapes of Wouvermans, Rembrandt and

(*Above left*) The water staircase of the Moorish Generalife, Granada, leading down from the slope above the house.

(*Above right*) Two views from Humphry Repton's Red Book of Bayham Abbey showing (*top*) the original landscape and (*below*) the 'naturalistic' landscape with a new lake and castle devised by Repton.

Hobbema. However much artifice was involved in constructing and designing Picturesque landscapes the desired end result was the appearance of nature's unguided hand having been at work, serendipitously influenced by the structure of Baroque painterly composition. Here was art imitating nature imitating art.

However much sense that seemed to make for nearly the next two centuries, it was only one orthodoxy in the longer history of landscape. There was the metaphor, the Zen abstraction and the ambiguity of Japan; the preoccupation with water, axiality, highly formalized geometry and intimations of Paradise of Islam; the *yin-yang* interpenetration of naturalism into geometric structure of China; the age-old formations of fields, strips, paddies and terraces of vernacular agriculture all over the world. Here were rich visual, cultural and aesthetic sources waiting to be plundered, adapted and given

Gertrude Jekyll's home and garden, Munstead Wood, designed by Edwin Lutyens. This garden combines a softly formal layout with chromatic planting themes.

new meanings in late-twentieth-century landscape.

In the West, as scholarly research had shown, landscapes by mid-eighteenth-century amateurs such as Henry Hoare at Stourhead had followed an iconographic programme: Hoare's was an allusion to Virgil's *Aeneid* in the sequence and layout of the garden structures and features of the landscape. William Hamilton laid out Painshill as a sequence of incidents, buildings and views down his Cobham valley. The earlier remodellings of formal landscapes by William Kent, he who according to Walpole 'leaped the fence and saw all Nature was a Garden', had been composed on a basis similar to stage-set design, incorporating structures alluding to revered antique remains. In this proto-Picturesque phase, landscape was about modified nature providing an integral setting for a succession of allusive and visual experiences: classical and cerebral rather than romantic and Picturesque.

These men had taken an entirely different approach from earlier French designers such as Le Nôtre, whose vast château landscapes were expressive more than anything of man's dominance over nature. These heroic landscape represented the first point at which landscapes became more significant in

(*Far left*) J.C.A. Alphand's Parc des Buttes-Chaumont of 1863 took the basic Paxton formula of swirling and winding roads and water to a dramatic extreme with these artificial crags overlooking a placid lake.

extent and character than the architecture which they surrounded – even so grand a structure as Versailles. Formed by the carving of great geometric slices in the form of *ronds-points* and radiating rides through heavily planted forest, they were designed for the ritual of hunting, the formal parterres around the great house decorating the immediate foreground. Their precursor, the compartmentalized garden of the Italian Renaissance, had established a set of conventional elements: parterres, allees, waterworks, hedges, sculpture, stairways, groves, pergolas, arbours. These formed a harmony of geometry and order, and were in a sense an externalization of the rooms of the house to which they provided a humanistic accompaniment.

All these represented alternative attitudes to nature, conditioned by the local cultures and climates and topographies whence they were developed. Seen as one of these phases in the history of landscape, the Picturesque tradition became merely one more possible source. If some contemporary landscape designers have not accepted that the Picturesque is now merely part of the contemporary landscape designer's baggage and have set their face firmly against it, this is because it has held such unchallenged sway for so long.

Changes in scope

The English Picturesque landscape and its developments had been designed for landowners, whether the country magnate clients of Repton or the public bodies for whom Paxton, Alphand and Olmsted had worked. In the 1950s and 1960s it gradually became clear that the scope of landscape design had changed. Small-scale private landscape or garden design continued, of course. But with a history of great landscaped estates, public parks, botanical gardens and enormous nature-conservancy projects, the profession of landscape architecture saw itself as operat-

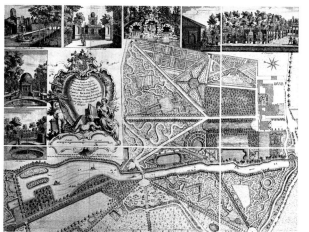

William Kent's layouts for the gardens at Chiswick House combine formalism, in the shape of controlled axes and vistas, with a degree of naturalism, in the form of winding internal paths and an irregular stretch of water.

Claude le Lorrain's *Aeneas at Delos*, one of the visual sources for views at Stourhead, Wiltshire, where the literary iconography is based on the sixth book of Virgil's *Aeneid*.

ing on a grander, more public scale than the flowered walks and shrub planting of suburban gardens. Until recently most landscape designers would have been slightly embarrassed at having it widely known that they had specified flowers in their landscape schemes.

The clients to match this new image began to appear in the heady rush of commercial and city development around the world. The new patrons were corporations and, as the problems of urban life increasingly impinged on them, local and municipal government bodies. Their motives had little to do with visual quality: rather, they were prosaic and functional, and ranged from a wish to add image to corporate buildings and town centres, through a response to political pressures from sectional interest groups, to a desire to ameliorate the visual and social poverty of the inner city. In some cases landscape designers have worked in close participation with local community groups. In addition, the new landscape often has to have a multiplicity of roles, incorporating such functions as entertainment and play.

Such motives, and the urban nature of the late twentieth century, together with the enormous pressures of real-estate values, have meant that much contemporary landscape design has been of a relatively modest scale. These exigencies and the reluctance of clients to spend much on upkeep made it inevitable that the criterion for designs and choice of materials had to be that of low maintenance. It was fortunate that the fashion for the Japanese garden sanctioned hard landscape in hard materials.

There have been exceptions to this: in the enormous scale of the landscape of civil engineering, the polders of the Netherlands, reservoirs, motorways, extractive industries, reclamation areas and huge national parks all over the world. All of these have produced responses from landscape designers, but invariably they have been attempts to recreate nature or at least a simulacrum of the nature which people would have liked to see there in the first place.

New relationships

What has changed too is the hitherto almost invariable relationship between architecture and landscape. That is not to say that much landscape is not still added on to buildings as an afterthought, the traditional complaint of landscape designers everywhere. But in an increasing number of cases the

Oosterpolder dyke after draining, seeding and settlement. Here is an unselfconsciously formal landscape created on the basis of real-estate allocations rather than design values and yet immensely evocative.

function of landscape is to ameliorate poor-quality environments and undistinguished architecture. In other cases architects work to master-plans devised by landscape designers; in still others, such as the NMB Bank in Amsterdam, the design of the whole complex has been a collaborative effort between all members of the design team; while in those such as George Hargreaves's central city park for San Jose, landscape is an entity in itself which makes reference in its planning to local natural pedestrian routes, and also to the cultural context of San Jose.

The designer landscape

Because of the redefinition of 'natural' elements in landscape, the consequent diminishing need for horticultural knowledge and the relatively weak position of landscape designers (in theory), a number of designers, architects and environmental artists, among them Bernard Tschumi, Emilio Ambasz, SITE, Elyn Zimmerman, Robert Smithson and Richard Long, seized the initiative in innovative landscape. They have not necessarily been troubled by the old internal problems and have taken on board a range of ideas and concepts from their own design disciplines. However much this tendency may be resented by licensed landscape architects, it has enriched and broadened the experience and meaning of landscape.

Earthworks: environmental art

One of the most liberating influences on contemporary landscape design has been the work of environmental artists. In a curious way it has been a reversal of the influence of the eighteenth-century pattern, when landscape designers such as Kent and Repton sought to design on the principles of composition and on the basis of the visual models provided by seventeenth-century landscape painters. It has raised a number of new questions for landscape designers about the relationship between art and landscape. In many cases, however seriously they are felt, these are merely demarcation problems, echoing the 'arts versus sciences' debate which has been going on in architecture for the last century. As in that argument, landscape is differentiated and elevated by its extra dimension of working functionally and ecologically, at the same time providing an enclosing, temporal, sequential experience rather than an empirical one.

Yet there have been visual and theoretical lessons to be learned from the work of artists taking a large-scale landscape environment as their canvas or clay and moulding or shaping it, giving it new meaning and significance. This is not the same thing as landscape designed to accommodate art, such as at Grizedale Forest in the English Lake District, a natural forest landscape which is gradually being populated by large-scale artworks made, in most cases, from natural materials. A more classic version of the type is Hans Lutz's landscape at the Max Planck research centre at Stuttgart, which has works of modern sculpture placed around it. A sensitive landscape in the Picturesque tradition, it is not particularly integrated with the artworks; rather, they have been appropriately positioned in the fashion of an open-air art gallery, or an updating of the classical tradition of sculpture in an arcadian setting, here without the dimension of classical symbolic meaning.

Environmental art, on the other hand, takes existing locations and by adding to them with a variety of artefacts and temporary structures completely changes their qualities and provides people with alternative ways of experiencing and understanding the normally banal spaces which they use every day. Christo, for example, moved from wrapping buildings to creating his enormously long *Running Fence* across the Arizona desert. Like later schemes it consisted of brightly-coloured fabric hung from a system of cables and poles running on an arbitrary route across the barren landscape. It was erected, photographed extensively and then dismantled. Not an attempt at landscape design, what it did was to provide a new way of thinking about the conventional relationships between natural materials and formations and the man-made, man-designed world.

Many land artists are preoccupied with the fundamental forces of nature. Gary Dwyer's *My Fault* project attempted to establish a language which charted the movement of a section of the San Andreas Fault at the linear valley of the Elkhorn

Hans Lutz and Partners' landscape for the Max Planck Institute, Stuttgart, a setting for appropriately placed works of art.

Scarp. His scheme, using the ancient Celtic Ogham script, which is composed of short lines scratched at various angles to a long determining line, was to lay along the fault a sequence of giant Ogham symbols in eight-foot-wide fibrous erosion-control matting. A tape of a sound work composed by a follower of John Cage would be played each sunset and when a seismic tremor occurred the sound of the earthquake would be recorded. As the earth on either side of the fault moved at a different pace the cross-lines of the Ogham script would realign, forming new words along the ordering line of the fault. Thus would the earth be enabled to speak.

Walter De Maria's *The Lightning Field* of 1971–7 near Quemado, New Mexico, had 400 five-cm/two-inch-diameter 6-metre/20-feet-high stainless steel poles set up in a regular 67-metre/220-foot grid one mile wide east to west and one kilometre long north to south. The poles gleam enigmatically in the desert, but when storm clouds gather they act as lightning conductors in this region of frequent electric storms, creating a symphony of lightning.

In a similar tradition is the work of the British environmental artist Andy Goldsworthy, who has moved from creating miniature or small-scale forms from found local materials such as leaves, stone, ice and timber to producing large earth-forming designs in which the basically ordered structure of natural objects is imprinted on the earth on a large scale. One of these consisted of circles of standing ice-blocks carved from the polar ice-cap and located precisely at the North Pole, the circle having to do with prehistoric megalithic structures, the shape of the universe and the earth, its alignment with the centre of the earth and its temporary nature, subject to the inevitable change wrought by nature over time.

Dwyer's design represented a line of thinking which argued that the artist's role was to respond to the vast, unmanageable, hidden forces of the earth. Artists such as Robert Smithson and Richard Long

created large-scale enigmatic forms in the landscape: Smithson's *Spiral Jetty*, in the Great Salt Lake, a very large spiral made from local stones and boulders, has been eroded, as intended, by the action of the sea and is now under water, visible only from an aircraft or the local headland. Michael Heitzer's *Pictorial Hills*, a series of enormous stylized insects and animals formed from earth mounding and selective planting and laid out on the hills near Ottawa, Illinois, is similarly softened by the action of nature. Like its source, the ancient giant diagrams in the Peruvian desert of beasts and geometric patterns, this ensemble can be properly made out only from the air: a kind of cosmic diagram, only the immediately local section of which is visible; the whole is apparent only to birds, aeronauts and, presumably, the spirits of the place.

Equally influential on some contemporary landscape designers has been the work of minimalist environmental artists. Not entirely surprisingly, the Zen rock and gravel garden has been an important influence, in its use of found forms, its cryptic meaning and its function of promoting contemplation. The American artist Carl Andre, for example, uses boulders, timber baulks and industrial 'found' materials arranged in strict geometric order

Andy Goldsworthy's ice sculpture at the North Pole, which lasted just as long as the elements (which it partly signifies) allowed.

and located variously in galleries and existing landscapes. As Peter Walker, who has been influenced by Andre, argues, 'Minimalism also resurrects the notion of spiritual meaning. Until recently contemporary gardens have been functional and sometimes beautiful, but not meaningful . . . Minimalism, with its emphasis on reduction to an essence, is one approach towards achieving mystery.'

On a different, ironic and witty line the work of SITE, the environmental artists/architects, has long sought to blur and make enigmatic the boundaries between everyday events and architecture and art and in so doing to heighten the observer's awareness of his immediate situation.

Deconstruction

The influence of Deconstructionism, originally a process of criticism but, like Structuralism several decades before, also seen as a philosophical base for design, lies partly behind the designs of Martha Schwartz and Alexandre Chemetoff, and quite explicitly behind Bernard Tschumi's Parc de la Villette in the northwest of Paris, with its arbitrary superimposition of three different ordering systems: lines, surfaces and points. Tschumi wrote, 'Each represents a different and autonomous system (or text) whose superimposition on another makes impossible any "composition", maintaining differences and refusing ascendancy to any privileged system or organizing element.'

Myth, metaphor and narrative

Some of the new issues stem from landscape's mythic and symbolic dimensions. Eden and Paradise were the first acts of Creation. Many designers have seen the possibility of translating that, as many land artists have done, into the notion that landscape is emblematic of the cosmic order and of the overwhelming forces of nature.

Kenchiro Ikehara's memorial landscape near Lake Caliraya, Manila, deploys such totemic references. Its 300-metre/1000-ft long symbolic path, the central axis for people who have come to remember the dead, runs straight up and over the contours to 'disappear up into the sky and into the heavens', explains Ikehara. And in one section is a series of 'global direction beams', stone markers planted in the earth around a stone table pointing through the earth to the cities of the world which they represent.

Symbolism takes a number of forms. Sir Geoffrey Jellicoe's later landscapes have been designed with post-Jungian symbolic intentions, with intimations of the collective unconscious of forms and the universal responses which they evoke.

Cultural contexts

For other designers the central theme is that meaning in landscape cannot be invented but has to derive from the locality's cultural roots, that landscape of any quality and depth needs a meaning which belongs to the cultural spirit of the past – not as a pastiche but as a unified ensemble of contemporary metaphors.

For example, the Grupo de Diseño's Parque Tezozomoc, a representation of the original Mexico Valley, was intended to provide the local people, almost all rootless immigrants, with a sense of place. As the poet Thomas Cavillo, a collaborator in the design, put it: 'Only in silence and solitude can we regain those dreams . . . and build, plan a space, sow trees, pile mountains, sail in the memory of a lake, run through the forests, hear and see whatever we want, name the paths, discover the symbols which have hitherto been concealed behind the locked cabinets of the museum, touch the serpent which makes waves and changes into a bird of rock, touch the stones which were touched, follow the boundary line of the face of a god. . . . To know who we are, to listen to the echo of a voice which sounds strangely like our own. This is the physical memory of our landscape.'

So, too, in Dani Freixes and Vicente Miranda's Parque del Clot, extensive elements of the vast old building originally on the site are retained, and in most cases transformed by subtle visual devices which have meaning for the landscape but also serve as a hint of the original context of the place. Much of the current work of George Hargreaves in the US is also designed on the basis of cultural memory, such as his San Jose Plaza.

Multivalence

Hargreaves's designs make reference to the work of (largely minimalist) three-dimensional and environmental artists whose work is site-specific, that is, generated by the context or form or spirit of their setting. His Fiddler's Green amphitheatre at Englewood, Colorado, is marked by great concentric half-rings in red gravel alternating with the sloping layers of grass in the bowl, and at the Villa Zapu at Napa, California, he has marked the hillside around the house, guest-house and pool with waving bands of drought-resistant grasses on which the sharp angular forms of the white buildings and random stands of local trees have been positioned. At one level this is an arbitrary, somewhat minimalist diagram placed on the local topography, echoing the acute forms of the architecture. At another it represents the plan view of the contour planting in the surrounding agricultural area – a kind of cultural topography.

This reach of the new landscape attempts to take on board as many disparate sources as seem appropriate to create a multivalent landscape. The California-based Peter Walker has drawn from minimalist sculpture, land art, experiments in phenomenology and painting. Apart from the need for a landscape to be a gift to society as a whole, as well as meeting the

needs of the client, his argument is for both an internal order and structure – such as music has – and a conceptual strength: 'Without . . . internal order, the work of landscape becomes invisible, blending into the continuum we call the landscape . . . Being appropriate or pleasant is not sufficient to sustain interest . . . if it is to be seen, it must have something to say or be about, perhaps several things at once.'

The classic order

One of the arguments behind Post-Modernist architecture's strong move in the direction of the classical tradition was that it was comprehensible by ordinary people. Ricardo Bofill's Taller de Arquitectura had applied this to the scale of the city: 'Block, street, grid, square – urban grid deliberately, simply orthogonal, like the layout of all cities in the past from Hippodamus to Cerda, from la Valette right up to New York . . . It is only through the use of this simple mechanism that we can dominate the city dynamic with differentiated yet egalitarian spaces.' Lurking behind the tradition of classicism is a profound belief in proportion and order as expressed by number and geometry. In the design of the Aiguera Park at Benidorm, a long irregular strip following an old riverbed into the centre of the town, the basic geometry was founded 'on a series of multiple numbers derived from the square root of two. We designed and determined everything from the smallest paving-stones to the pilasters, as well as the lengths and widths of the designed spaces.'

The fundamentalist classic position is to do with the inherent order of Euclidean geometry, Cartesian space, with the numinous three-dimensional grid which underlies all things: so runs the general argument. By latching on to the cosmic geometry in his work man acquires virtue and creates objects, buildings and environments which are inherently in tune with the cosmos. It is rare for designers to put it quite that way, or as simplistically. Yet some designers clearly have this intention behind their work, which invariably is superficially labelled either classical or classic. As the history of landscape has shown, there has been nothing irrational in believing this true of nature as well.

The new relationship with architecture

There will always be landscapes which are intended as settings for architecture, whether formal, Virgilian, Picturesque, Deconstructed or whatever. But other possibilities exist, such as at the NMB Bank, Amsterdam, where landscape designers were equal partners in the preliminary design team of an unusual building in which the landscape is an integral element; and at Robson Square, which uses the landscape as the building's cladding, with a sheet of water as a roof. More radical is Emilio Ambasz, who in a series of designs for houses and office buildings reverses the architectural convention of surrounding buildings with landscape by digging the accommodation into the earth. He then mounds over it a minimal, somewhat Brownean prairiescape, incised here and shifted up and down there, the shear lines edged by the glazing needed for the buildings to work as habitable spaces, and always he incorporates water, either as very formal shapes or as Brownean meanders.

The new landscape is fundamentally pluralist. It is divergent rather than convergent, multivalent rather than conforming to a universally agreed set of aesthetic values. This is in some ways an inevitable development for an art which is now put to such diverse uses – from small-scale commerce to large-scale recreation – and whose palette of permissible materials has become so extensive. It ranges from the use of flowering plants, hitherto held at arm's length,

through the gamut of conventional planting materials of widely differing climates and geologies to astroturf and gilded frogs from the local hardware store.

A central theme in the new landscape is the preoccupation with context and meaning. They have not been much in evidence in landscape theory of the last two hundred years. Yet they have often played an important part in the history of landscape design: consider the reflections of Paradise in Islamic gardens, the expressions of centralizing political power in seventeenth-century France, the hermetic and overt symbolism of much Italian Renaissance garden design and such a notable symbolic landscape as Bomarzo and the eighteenth-century dual Virgilian/ Claudian coding of Henry Hoare's eighteenth-century Stourhead.

The preoccupations and concerns now are with the design of landscape which is intended to be read not only at the level of visual composition, but at other levels as well. The new landscape design addresses the mind overtly, subconsciously, allusively, confrontationally, even ironically. It may be aimed primarily at the cognoscenti as self-conscious commentary on conventional approaches to landscape, or on traditional design principles as in the case of Schwartz and Tschumi, whose deliberate formal disjunctions negate established senses of order. Other, secondary layers may refer to cultural contexts, in the form taken by the Grupo de Diseño's Tezozomoc Park, Bernard Lassus's Garden of Returns at Rochefort, George Hargreaves's San Jose Plaza and in a different way Richard Haag's Gas Works Park. Lassus and Haag share another common interest, in minimal intervention, in which the new design takes the existing context, nudges it a little, adds here and there and slightly reorganizes it into a fresh revelation. In cases such as Ian Hamilton Finlay's Little Sparta, the sub-text may be a series of commentaries on the role of art in the public realm in the late twentieth century, or Sir Geoffrey Jellicoe's post-Jungian symbolism at Sutton Place and his design for the Moodey botanical gardens at Galveston – or, as in Emilio Ambasz's Folly, it may be hermetic and intensely personal.

Much of this has come about from a recognition that naturalistic landscape as practised in England since the eighteenth century is every bit as artificial as the formal landscape against which it had reacted. Naturalism still has a widespread ascendancy in the landscape world. But for the newly emerging landscape thinking it addresses only a narrow group of primarily practical problems, and is internally inconsistent in attempting to design nature. Intellectually it is profoundly unsatisfying.

The new landscape has also addressed physical context in a fresh way. However disapprovingly McHarg and his Penn School are viewed as having thoughtlessly reinforced the naturalistic approach, his insistence on ecological balances in landscape has been a major influence. So too has the teaching and writing of a group of people around Lawrence Halprin in thinking of landscape in somewhat Zen terms, as a sequence of carefully evoked sensual experiences, a combination of such elements as wind, water, sun, lightning, shade, heat, cold, sound, enclosure, form. Confusingly for the seeker after a single new landscape aesthetic, this direction may not necessarily preclude the knowing deployment of naturalistic visual passages.

Commentators on any of the arts have a vested interest in keeping things simple and reinforcing the notion of a mainstream avant-garde – however contradictory that might seem. The new landscape currently defies that kind of convergence. Its patterns for the foreseeable future lie in an exploration of both the single theme taken to its extreme limits and of combinations of all themes. One thing that is clear is that landscape will no longer be a kind of grown-up, large-scale, rather severe version of the domestic garden.

The choice of landscape designs selected for this book is necessarily the author's, advised by a number of experts in the field. There were a number of preliminary criteria for selection. First, the landscapes had in some way to break new ground, or to be representative of particular directions and themes in contemporary landscape design of the last two decades. Second, they had to exhibit the difficult-to-define quality of design talent. Third, as far as possible, only one example of each designer's work was included. This means that some excellent landscapes have been left out and that some readers may be affronted by the exclusion of landscapes which they know and admire.

This is a book about design as much as landscape. Some of the landscapes chosen therefore either no longer exist or have declined from their original quality. In some cases this is because they were designed to last only a short time; sometimes it is simply because they have not been properly maintained. Almost all the built landscapes have changed as planting has grown and subsequent owners taken over, but the illustrations are as far as possible of the designers' original conceptions.

1 RESPONSES TO THE URBAN SCENE

The late-nineteenth-century concept of the Garden City has been honoured more frequently in the breach than in the observance, and has always been difficult to implement retrospectively in densely populated inner cities. Yet increasingly the social problems of the inner city, its socially inimical overcrowding, its divisive fast road systems, the need for community identity, have made the idea of landscape in the city increasingly desirable. In many cases, such as at Longfellow Garden in the Bronx, it was important that the design team worked with the local community, for that provided the hope, although no guarantee, that the new landscape would be cared for by the people who acted as the clients. Other cases, such as the pocket plaza off the busy commercial Wilshire Boulevard in Los Angeles, provide a tiny, humanizing respite in the relentless rush of downtown business. Response to exigent urban circumstances may also be on a grand scale, such as the Taller de Arquitectura's design for the Turia Gardens in a great dry riverbed running through the middle of Valencia, or Halprin's Seattle Freeway Park, an unexpected and imaginative use of freeway air rights. And in the rurban (rural/urban fringe) setting of the outskirts of Denver, Colorado, the SWA Group have produced an unexpected frame for the distant crags of the Rocky Mountains.

Harlequin Plaza, Denver, Colorado.

1.1

Allen Fong: Fong, Preston, Jung Associates

WILSHIRE PLAZA POCKET PARK

Los Angeles
1976

for Ketcham Peck & Tooley (C.L. Peck, contractor)

Fong, Preston, Jung Associates were commissioned by Ketcham Peck & Tooley to design a landscape on the roof of the underground car park adjoining their new 12-storey office block on mid-Wilshire Boulevard. The surrounding environment is a dense development of tall office and commercial buildings and the street is heavy with motor traffic. It is effectively a residual space, known colloquially in the landscape and architectural world as SLOAP – space left over after planning. In this case it was a tiny space, no more than 12 metres/40 ft wide and 18 metres/60 ft deep, flanked by tall buildings and overlooked by a ground-floor restaurant in the new building on the east.

The client intended that it should be used by the public, as a place to sit and read, to lunch or take a break in the sun – the site faces due south. Access was also needed to an office at the back and to a fire exit from the client's own building at the side.

The sidewalk outside the building and along a massive colonnade down the west side had been paved in brick, so Allen Fong made the decision to use the same bricks for all the hard elements in the scheme. This was partly a matter of maintaining continuity, partly because the scale of bricks provided a contrast to the massive buildings on either side and partly for reasons of relative economy and ease of maintenance.

As a signpost to this unexpected green interlude in a heavily commercialized street, Fong designed a circular banked fountain base protruding beyond the building line, with a standard half-dandelion fountain set in an array of concentric brick circles; shallow steps form a basin for the fountain's water.

The plan beyond the raised circular fountain is very simple: a line of fig trees runs along the white-painted brick wall of the adjoining office building and a circular built-up brick sitting area is sited at the back away from the traffic of the street. A tall brick wall closes off the rear of the site.

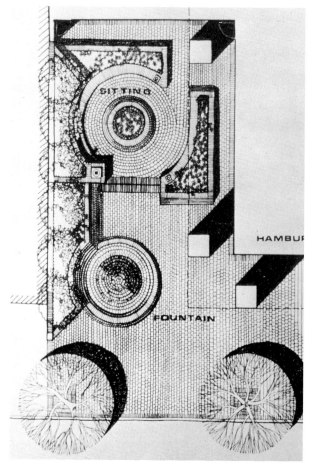

(***Top and opposite***) **Wilshire Plaza from the back (*top*) and from the street: a simple brick-clad ensemble of circles and squares and carefully clipped planting which can be viewed as either slotting humanely between two massive commercial developments, or making an elegant contribution to keeping them apart.**

(***Above***) **The plan reveals its functional simplicity: access was needed to the building on the right and to an office at the top left. There was a restaurant at ground level on the right and the local council was persuaded to allow the sidewalk to be clad in brick, visually extending the actual area and integrating it with the new building.**

(*Left and opposite*) **The fountain, set in a subtly designed circular basin of brick, serves as the street introduction to the space, backed by a dense range of fig-trees in raised beds along the outer edge of the plot.**

(*Above*) **The planter at the rear of the site echoes the predominant circular theme of the park.**

In order for the roots to be able to support the fig trees on this car-park roof the trees have been set in a raised planter. This, like other planters in the park, is filled with massed annuals and perennials which are changed regularly to accommodate seasonal variety and colour. The brick column supporting the restaurant's street sign is draped with climbing plants which help to resolve the visual problem caused by extending the planter into the sidewalk.

Rather than always build vertical walls, Fong chose to step much of the brickwork – especially for the two major circles and for the retaining wall of the planter supporting the row of fig trees. The effect is to soften the sharp geometric forms of the plan.

Wilshire Plaza pocket park is a refined example of what can be done in downtown commercial development. Fong has deployed a very simple range of materials and a palette of colours which relate to its scale. With plenty of unfussy sitting-out places, it is used extensively by lunchtime office workers in search of a bosky haven from the air-conditioned offices round about.

One of the earliest pocket parks, Wilshire has served as a model for a number of similar schemes in urban commercial settings. It has been successful because, although the park is dedicated to the public, unlike many parks in public ownership it is carefully maintained by the owners throughout the year.

1.2

Lawrence Halprin

SEATTLE FREEWAY PARK

Seattle, Washington
1976
for Seattle Park Commission

Following the publication of Lawrence Halprin's book *Freeways* in 1966, Seattle Park Commission asked him to develop his ideas in the context of a city park they proposed alongside Interstate 5. The freeway carved a north–south canyon through downtown Seattle, irrevocably cutting off one side, the financial district, from the other, a residential zone. Halprin's radical proposal was to create a more extensive landscape which in a sense ignored the freeway by building over it, thus connecting the two districts once again. The air rights over the freeway were owned by the public so that there were no land acquisition costs – and no loss of tax revenue to the city, which any other ground-based public landscape proposal would have entailed.

The 2.2-hectare/5.5-acre landscape stretches for 400 metres/1300 ft. It starts with an isolated garden bounded by a curving access ramp and crosses a road bridging the freeway, emerging into a big space surrounding a large formal office block and covering the freeway. At its north-east corner it runs under another road parallel with the freeway, under a high-level traffic ramp, and then north-east alongside this

road, up to the roof level of a large garage. It is an interweaving of landscape with complex access routes, entirely covering a block-length section of the main 10-lane freeway. The highest point in the landscape is 30 metres/90 ft above the lowest: the change in grades is sometimes significant.

Halprin describes his approach thus: 'The trick is to perceive the old freeway as part of the cityscape and tame it rather than complain about it.'

The consistent visual theme in the landscape is a sprawling irregular grouping of geometric forms in board-marked concrete, sometimes vertically striated, sometimes horizontally. In some cases they take the form of giant planters for trees and shrubs with heavy foliage, in others the deliberately artificial 'rockwork' for fountains. They are the primary structural background for a central water canyon

(*Left*) Plan of Seattle Freeway Park. The grid-iron of city streets has been crudely ignored by the traffic engineers' need to provide high-speed curvatures, turn-offs and then flyovers which brutally re-integrate automobiles into the pattern of everyday life. Halprin's design was original in dismissing the sacrosanct status of freeway routes; it calmly spreads itself across them.

SEATTLE FREEWAY PARK

Designed by Lawrence Halprin & Associates
For the City of Seattle
Washington State Highway Commission Department of Highways
R.C.Hedreen Company

(*Left*) The most dramatic feature of the landscape: the water canyon centrally located in the dead space between the north- and south-bound sections of the freeway below. The architectonic elements are cast pieces of striated concrete, here acting as man-made rock faces, elsewhere as pools, waterfalls, giant planters and armatures for foliage. Overall they serve as the simple consistent element in an otherwise heavily planted ensemble.

(*Above*) Aerial view from the north, with the landscape on top of the car park (*bottom left*) descending to ground level, under a flyover, over the main freeway and finally surrounding a curving slip-road off the freeway (*top*).

(*Left*) A section across the motorway: Halprin has creatively used the dead space separating the main carriageways of the freeway to insert the sculptured water canyon.

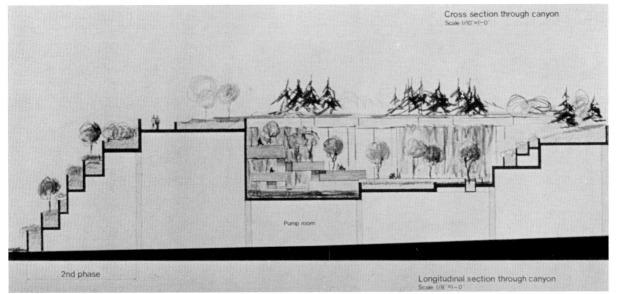

Cross section through canyon
Scale 1/10"=1'-0"

Pump room

2nd phase

Longitudinal section through canyon
Scale 1/8"=1'-0"

located over the dead space left between the two freeway carriageways. In other cases they project in an irregular array over the freeway, with trees and draping greenery providing motorists with a momentary hint that they are missing something green and unusual overhead. Trees planted in these overhanging structures also provide a screen against the winds created by the channelling effect of the freeway and its border of high buildings. At the south edge of the landscape deck the cubic concrete forms and their associated landscape step down right into the central reservation.

The surrounding area is concrete-and-steel cityscape with the concrete freeway canyon below. Halprin has deliberately turned his back on any temptation to create an artificial 'naturalness'. In various spots in the ensemble there are glazed openings with views of the cars streaming past below, reminding visitors that they are over a freeway, providing them with something like the reverse of the freeway driver's experience.

(*Left*) In winter, when fewer people are about, Halprin's water entirely changes character, from a summer place of noisy rushing streams and falls among which people can sit and splash into a serene ensemble of frozen calm in which the dark trees and grey concrete form a foundation for the random but often extraordinary operations of nature.

(*Top*) Halprin's use of water here and in other projects is designed so that people are encouraged to join in with it, play, get wet, clamber around and enjoy it. It is an aural experience as well: here the speed of the falling water is deliberately tuned not only to provide pleasure but to serve as a kind of white noise, blocking out the roar of the motorway.

(*Left*) The water canyon cascade, a noisy flurry of movement and sound as the water plunges from shelf to shelf and finally to the pool below. This is an unlikely experience for a downtown area, least of all between two carriageways of a freeway. What is ostensibly a collection of concrete shapes surrounded by planting has become a place of drama, in which it is possible for the visitor to become involved. Instead of putting up notices forbidding climbing, Halprin believes that the plainly visible danger is a much better protection against people taking silly risks. The increasingly stained concrete has developed its own version of a patina. The horizontal and vertical striations encourage different patterns of weathering.

Halprin has always used water extensively, and here, as in others of his projects, he has designed the water so that people can play around and in it. The water is deliberately dramatic, fast-moving down the rugged concrete, splashing into lower-level basins and then over their lips to yet more below, and changing direction all the while. It has more than a visual function, for its noise is intended to attenuate the ambient noise from traffic all around the site.

The 21-storey office block was built at the same time following a series of deals which relocated it from its original position to the north of its site to minimize shadows cast over the landscape. The roof of the building's parking garage was incorporated into the site. Its plaza overlooks the side of the canyon, which runs north–south and therefore gains as much light as possible, and the central reservation fortunately also runs in that direction. The centre-piece of the design, this is formed from board-marked concrete and is full of the noisy rush of water pouring from plateau to plateau, through and around the planting, down a large cascade at the north end – it is recirculated at a rate of 100,000 litres/ 28,000 gallons per minute. Much of the canyon looks too dangerous for people to play around but Halprin believes that the appearance of danger is protection in itself – better than insisting that the exciting concrete rockwork should be placed off-limits.

If Seattle Freeway Park has a unifying metaphor it is that of a peak and meadow mountain landscape. Halprin has planted rhododendrons, azaleas and

alders among the lower levels of the scheme, Douglas fir and upland trees in the higher zones. There is no formal street furniture; lighting is primarily floods on 30-metre/100-ft poles, providing a blanket cover of light rather than a multiplicity of fussy 'feature' lights.

The canyon is only one of a number of domains in the park. The southernmost domain is formed by a jumble of giant concrete planter boxes cascading down towards freeway level. There are quieter, more sylvan sections; others are quite architectural with splashes of the ubiquitous water in geometric watercourses. It is an episodic design – inevitable given the odd locations amongst the spaghetti-work of roadways. That also reflects the way the whole design evolved, a process of taking opportunities as the possibilities of using more pieces of land emerged.

1.3
Moore Perez Associates and Ron Filson

PIAZZA D'ITALIA
New Orleans, Louisiana
1980
For UIG

Piazza d'Italia is located in a commercial and industrial area of New Orleans. It was intended to provide the local Italian community with an identity in this city where other ethnic cultures predominate. An office block occupied one corner of the site, together with several old warehouses and the community's headquarters building. The completed design is effectively a circular plaza carved out from the middle of a city block of standard commercial development with three radial entrances from the streets outside. One takes the form of a great multi-coloured triumphal arch: opposite is a wide wedge-shaped avenue, one of its street corners marked by a campanile. The main feature is a group of trees in planters behind a steel pergola, roughly in the formation of a Roman temple, angled deliberately asymmetrically from any obvious axis in the avenue.

In plan the dominant visual theme is a series of concentric rings formed by brick paving, granite setts and black slate recycled from a street reconstruction nearby. It is as if the whole block has been laid out in concentric ring formation and the buildings then replaced, leaving the circular geometry visible in the centre and in the three open access routes. The strength of the circular patterning indicates to passers-by in the street that something is going on at the epicentre.

The architectural centrepiece is a large curved screen surrounding the east rim of the central circle. Moore designed it in a Roman manner with Corinthian and Ionic columns, stainless steel capitals – some with neon collars – and mouldings in the big central arch picked out with neon tubing. A less elaborate screen stands in front of this. It is painted terracotta and has variously stainless steel Doric columns and Tuscan columns formed by what are effectively shower-heads.

Water comes from a variety of unexpected sources: the bases of the pilasters around the rear screen, the Doric capitals and several jets in the main fountain. Water also jets from the mouths of a pair of

three-dimensional portraits of Moore's own face on either side of an arch in the inner screen.

Some of the architectural detailing is authentic enough. But as an ensemble this is not reproduction classical architecture – the use of unexpected materials such as stainless steel, neon and concrete, and the deliberate mis-juxtaposition of formal classical elements and their asymmetrical disposition indicate this quite plainly. Moore and his team – actually two separate practices – wanted to incorporate truck windscreen wipers to make it clear that this was the twentieth century, but he was told that he couldn't be serious.

(*Above left*) **A pergola in the general formation of a Roman temple in the short entrance avenue on the north side.**

(*Above*) The centrepiece of the piazza, a waterscape setting for ironically detailed classical 'fragments' with the map of Italy formed by many layers of contrasting stone.

(*Right*) The candy-striped lectern is positioned on the map of Sicily for the annual St Joseph's Day festivities.

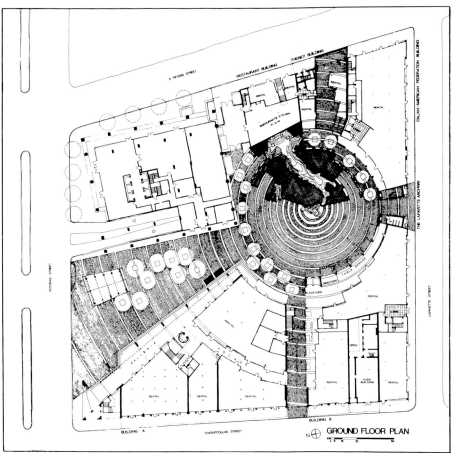

The effect is to create a group of three-dimensional theatre sets through which the surrounding environment can be seen and which provide a setting for the fountain: rather as do the fragments of classical ruins still standing in Italy today.

The water feature, designed in consultation with the local Italian community, is a representation of the topography of Italy in alternate black and white layers of stone rather like a crude contour model. From the centrepiece arched recess, where the 'contours' build up steeply, water pours down the series of steps to the main pool – representing the Adriatic and Tyrrhenian seas – and around the open curved corridor between the two architectural screens. The water channels from the source (representing the Alps) stand for the three great rivers of Italy, the Arno, Po and Tiber. That is all apparent from reading the plan of the scheme. At ground level the first impression is of a series of irregular layered levels along and over which the water moves. The water works not as a set of conventional pools and rivulets but rather as a thin coating to the granite, slate and brick hard surfacing only a few inches below. Moore has cited the Trevi Fountain as an inspiration, with its rough rocks, occasional jets, thin sheets of water pouring from the edge of basins and shallow pools.

The local community is largely Sicilian in origin and the representation of Sicily forms the centre of the whole concentric ground-patterning. Once a

(*Left*) **The concentric rings form the ordering visual structure for the whole scheme, which is set in a back-lot in the middle of a New Orleans city block. The rear screen, complete with inscriptions, consists of a series of variations on the Corinthian order, and echoes the ruins at Hadrian's villa. The two foreground screens are a mix of Doric (in stainless steel) and a primitive square order which is almost Egyptian.**

(*Above*) **Plan: the map of Italy, with Sicily at the centre of the pattern of concentric rings which underlie the whole scheme. The broad north entrance 'avenue' with the Roman temple pergola is on the left, with a Post-Modern triumphal arch off the street to the south and public amenities to the east.**

year, on St Joseph's Day, the Italian community holds a public festival and the local mayor gives his address from a podium on this centrepiece, home as it were from home.

For designers the Piazza d'Italia contains a multitude of architectural references: the Trevi Fountain, Hadrian's Villa, the gateways of Schinkel – as well as the more obvious references to Italy and its architectural heritage understood by the local community – and the kinds of public spaces to be found in traditional Italy. Another local, commercial, brash American tradition is denoted by the use of neon,

and a new order invented by Moore nicknamed by the design team the Delicatessen Order, which invokes the imagery of sausages hanging in a shop window.

The Piazza is of course both serious and ironic at the same time. Its internal jokes and ironic references are like Mannerist design, there for whoever can understand them. They add a richness to the visible forms of a space which serves its function as a notable landmark and focus for the local Italian community, a heterogeneous combination of all the three-dimensional arts and urban design.

(*Above*) Classical columns and detailing outlined by neon tubing.

(*Opposite*) The classical centrepiece forms the source for the Alps at the head of the contour map of Italy; ostensibly a solemn traditional classical façade, its inherent pomposity is deflated by the lighting, based on everyday commercial neon. The central arch encloses not some deity or important figure but the upper level of what from this view appear to be random layers of stone covered with sheets of gently trickling water.

(*Right*) From this view the contour map of Italy reads as an irregular sculptural layering of stones of different kinds wandering through a group of three-dimensional stage-set classical screens.

1.4
The SWA Group

HARLEQUIN PLAZA
Greenwood Village, Colorado
1983
for John Madden Company

The Sausalito-based SWA Group were called in by the John Madden Company and its architects Gensler & Associates to create a public plaza between a pair of angled mirror-glass speculative office buildings to be completed in Greenwood Village, Colorado. The development was in a standard suburban office development corridor 20 miles south of Denver.

The one-acre space was actually the top of a two-storey car park dotted with vents and chillers, most of them around 3 metres/10 ft high. Substantial enough to carry people, the roof could accommodate landscape loadings only in a 12-metre/40-ft-wide strip down the middle of the 50 × 100-metre/ 160 × 320-ft space. The one positive factor was that the space opened out to an unobstructed view of the Rocky Mountains.

The main elements of SWA's brief were to design a plaza for public functions, to accentuate the views of the mountains and to mitigate the visual effect of the mechanical equipment. On the face of it, this was the kind of *post-hoc* problem which landscape architects frequently face: a cosmetic, patching-up job on a site whose form and scale are irretrievably predetermined.

Instead of filling in the space in a conventionally axial fashion SWA saw that the problems of the site presented opportunities, providing unexpected

reference points from which to work. There were several planning issues to solve: the relationship of the plaza to the mirror-glass buildings which framed it on either side, and the long axial view of the Rockies. The indented entrances of the buildings faced one another and it made sense to create a direct path between the two. In theory the view across this axis should have been repeated endlessly in the mirror entrance doors of the two buildings. At the same time anything on the plaza would be mirrored back and forth between the two mirror walls in the same way.

Another factor was that the view to the Rockies was one of immense scale: there is almost no development between the plaza and the often snow-clad mountains blocking the horizon. A radical, abstract solution was called for which responded to the strangeness of scale of the vista and the disorientation created by the mirrored flanking walls.

(Left) Model: the plaza is bisected by the soft landscape slit which follows the line of permissible floor loadings; it is edged with great magenta slabs pushed arbitrarily to each side and cut in the middle on the axis of the mirror-image entrances to the two office buildings lining the sides of the space.

(*Above*) A giant hand, fancifully perhaps from the vast spaces in the far distance, has placed various geometric elements in the giant patterned terrazzo floor, where a single tree represents a token soft landscape element in deference to the greater landscape beyond. The sloping rectangular solid houses an air-vent which local building laws insisted had to be 3 metres/10 ft above floor level (actually the roof of the car park underneath).

(*Right*) The plaza paving slides across the central landscape slit.

Looking down the long axis of the plaza across to the vast expanse of the mountains, it is as if some giant hand has arbitrarily disposed a series of precisely engineered components with mysterious functions on a super-scaled harlequin pattern surface. SWA paved most of the plaza in a diamond-patterned terrazzo, encased the vents and chiller units in cubes of mirror-glass with slanting roofs and, following the zone which could carry landscape loads, cut a long slit and laid a narrow channel of water with regularly spaced fountains; beds of annual plants were set on either side.

The soft landscape slit has slightly converging walls of red-painted aluminium cladding which have, as it were, been casually wedged down each side, sloping in opposite directions. At each end a great sloping triangular mirror reflects the line of the fountain trench – but at a slight angle, avoiding a repercussive mirror effect up and down the slit. The recessed entrances of the two mirror-glass buildings are each half-way down the plaza, and here SWA cut through the red walls and ran the plaza paving as a bridge over the slit, arranging a small group of trees near the crossing. White cylinders of different heights set in small raised areas of grass were grouped in the entrance recesses of the two buildings. Reflected in the mirror walls behind, they have the effect of small truncated forests.

(*Above*) The walled landscape slit, with its ironic flowers and fountained water-channel. The effect is less of a false perspective than a deliberate disorientation, enhanced by the hard-edged metal cladding.

(*Right*) Closed on two sides by mirror-glass buildings, the plaza overlooks the snowcapped Rocky Mountains at its open end. The central slit is terminated at each end by a great, slightly sloping triangular mirror, which concentrates the very small-scale soft landscape scene. The mirror cubes with sloping tops are a response to the mirrored environment on either side and actually disguise in an imaginative way the air-handling units from the car park underneath. Dividing the plaza into two creates sufficiently intimate spaces in front of the two buildings for public activities and reduces the scale of the whole space.

(*Right*) The slit is an apparently arbitrary slice through the middle of the harlequin-patterned plaza, with two long walls sloping in opposite directions and converging at one end of the plaza.

Capitalizing as it were on the disorientation which mirror walls create, and repeating the material in the chiller unit cladding and again in the triangular mirrors at each end of the soft landscape slit, SWA have built on the visual scenario with which they were presented, exaggerating the pervasiveness of mirrors, but denying the disorientating effect of two opposing mirrors by driving the red walls down the middle of the space.

The slit operates at different levels. First, in a real-estate sense, its walls divide the site into two, giving each of the buildings a plaza of its own. Secondly, it provides a gesture in the direction of conventional landscape by incorporating a fairly traditional fountained canal and flowers, which are more the province of gardeners than of landscape designers. At the same time the soft landscape slit leads the eye of the observer out of the plaza into the vast wilderness beyond.

The striking, fantastical quality of the design is in sharp contrast to the suburban to semi-rural anonymity of the area. It works as an unexpected, slightly disorientating oasis, whose enigmatic geometric shapes in painted aluminium and mirror glass have a curious de Chirico-like quality. It is also an oasis in the sense that it functions as a public space well used: the Denver Symphony Orchestra has performed there.

(*Left*) The main axis across the plaza between the entrances of the two buildings: the slab walls to the landscape slit are simply cut through and the terrazzo plaza floor simply carried over the bridge across the slit.

(*Above*) Detail of the harlequin-patterned floor.

1.5
Taller de Arquitectura
JARDINS DE TURIA
Valencia, Spain
1981–85
for the City of Valencia

Ricardo Bofill's Taller de Arquitectura (Architecture Workshop) was commissioned by the city of Valencia to prepare a master-plan for the former bed of the river Turia. Until 1956 the river had curved through the centre of Valencia to the sea. But a serious flood finally persuaded the authorities to divert the waterway around the city, leaving a wide disused riverbed crossed by many bridges. Without water its effect was of an eyesore slashing through the middle of the city.

The Taller designers first of all looked at the form and structure and the workings of the whole city through which the river had acted as a major physical intervention, in some cases determining the pattern of roads and in others serving as an irregular cut-off for road layouts orientated to other elements such as

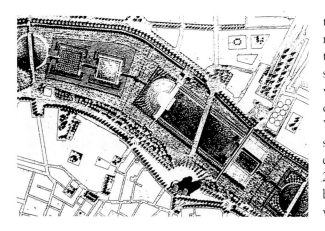

the port and seashore. At the same time, eyesore or not, the riverbed was in a sense the spinal column of the city. That called for a strongly unified design solution, whose main axes were clearly defined and whose planting scheme would emphasize the unity of the eight-kilometre/five-mile-long project. Water had to play an important part, not only as a symbol of the old river but as part of the design ensemble. The riverbed, effectively a great swathe 200 metres/220 yds wide, was bounded on each side by roads or boulevards overlooking the retaining walls of the river-banks and crossed at a variety of

(*Left above*) **The master plan, with the route of the landscape following the old Turia riverbed through Valencia to the seaport (*bottom right*).**

(*Left below*) **Detailed plan of the Taller de Arquitectura proposals incorporating the existing bridges.**

angles by bridges connecting major traffic arteries on either side.

In previous projects the Taller had already begun to develop a typology for city landscapes which emphasized simplicity and maintenance, a natural classical hierarchy and geometry, together with the use of plant material native to the area. This they put into practice in the present scheme. The design starts to the west of the city with a large lake surrounded by an orchard. It serves as a reservoir for irrigation and a place for water-sports and leisure activities. On the course of the riverbed north-east and then south-

(*Above*) The centrepiece of the long garden, an ensemble of neo-classical architecture and landscape.

(*Left*) Behind the freestanding loggia the background of perimeter foliage serves to form boundaries to the individual compartments.

east there is a series of formal landscapes and urban spaces leading eventually to the old port and waterfront.

The basic design is of a great linear pine forest planted right up to the old river-banks out of which have been scooped a number of formal spaces: some garden spaces, some settings for buildings and some settings for public activities such as large festivals, spectacles, fiestas and carnivals. These outdoor rooms offer a succession of public uses. There are orangeries, botanical gardens, fruit gardens, cultural spaces and parks for sport. In smaller clearings are orderly arrangements of paths, plazas, promenades, belvederes, playing-fields and meeting-spaces. The scheme is based on the formality of the Mediterranean garden with the additional element of public space.

There is no grass. In this climate it tends to dry out patchily, so ground surfaces are gravel, compacted earth and pavement. Underplanting is boxwood, rose, laurel, rosemary and thyme. For the rest the planting is almost entirely trees, comparatively low in height and resistant to sun, poor soil and drought. The primary effect is of a contrast of light and dark tones of green throughout the year, with seasonal additions of colour from fruit-trees and shrubs.

The pinewoods act as an enclosing background, effectively filling the whole of the riverbed. They serve as a buffer between the meandering boundaries of the site and the formal compositions within them. The transition from formal spaces to forest is achieved by using other native plant species such as cypress, orange trees, palms and olive trees arranged in geometric and hierarchical order. For the whole design is based on a very strict geometry: 'Geometry defines the path of the viewer and the direction of the space; it transforms chaos and obscurity into order and clarity . . . The geometric layout acquires a structural value of support and can be decomposed into more complex geometries on a smaller scale down to the most minute details,' say the architects. The function of the layout is to capture the axial

(*Above*) The piers of one of the old bridges become an active element in the formal ensemble.

connotations of the surrounding city and create master lines for the landscape, providing an internal order and dividing the series of spaces into logical parts.

Where the bridges cross, the Taller has sometimes used them as part of the ordering structure and sometimes simply let them fly over the formal composition on the bed of the river below. Around the main bridge, the Puente de Serrano, is a circular form with a theatre-plaza and a big circular pool.

Architectural elements form an important part of the whole composition. As always in the work of the Taller these have been designed in a formal Post-Modern classical style whose source is Roman rather than Greek and whose design is redolent of a cultural interpretation of the Mediterranean past rather than an attempt to recreate it.

(*Above*) The formality of the architectural elements is echoed by the hierarchy of plant size and species. Behind, palm trees are used to define the edge of the circular pool laid under the old bridge.

1.6
Lee Weintraub

LONGFELLOW GARDEN

165th Street and Longfellow Avenue, New York City

1984

for the South East Bronx Community Organization

Lee Weintraub created the half-acre Longfellow garden when he was working as director of the Open Space Program at the New York City Department of Housing Preservation and Development (HPD). It is in the Hunt's Point Triangle of the South Bronx, a depressed minority area of five- and six-storey apartments. This urban landscape is the outcome of local community action: the South East Bronx Community Organization wanted HPD to create a place of serenity with good design and decorative planting rather than the cheap, no-maintenance asphalted space traditionally provided by public authorities. It was to be a space usable by the whole range of local residents, from children through

(*Below*) The upper terrace of Longfellow Garden, designed for local residents to plant their own choice of flowers in their own square plots. Around the perimeter is seating for people to sit and watch in traditional public-garden fashion. The next terrace, several feet below, is taken up with the Post-Modern pergola and its exaggerated Egyptian/bulbous Doric columns and open steel roof.

(**Right**) Plan: the local residents' flower garden terrace (**right**), pergola terrace (**centre**) and the lower children's play terrace (**left**).

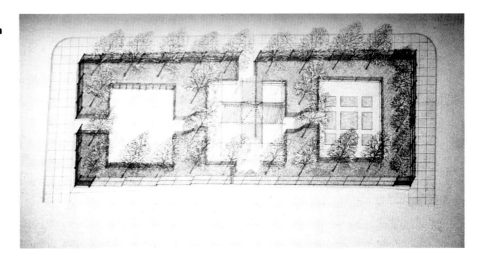

gardeners to old people who simply wanted to sit. The local community organization had identified a suitable derelict lot on the corner of Longfellow Avenue and 165th Street. After negotiations with the City authorities, Weintraub started work on the design with the architects Jose Cheing and Ellen Bensen, in close consultation with the community group. Weintraub argued that the people who live near or use a park often have clearer insight than designers are willing to give them credit for.

Longfellow is one of several collaborations between Weintraub and SEBCO. It was designed when HPD was going through a phase in which it was prepared to accept the notion that public landscapes needed high-quality materials and planting.

The deal struck with the local group was that, in return for being given the site and the landscape, it would take on responsibility for keeping it clean and tidy and for carrying out all maintenance. In a downmarket locality that made sense, despite the risk that it depended on local support continuing year after year.

The sloping site, bounded on three sides by streets, is very simply arranged in three brick-paved terraces linked by stairs and surrounded by honey-locust trees, with an internal grid of small-leaved linden trees intended to be clipped to reflect the geometry of the terraces. The underplanting is lush rhododendrons and azaleas with ground cover of *Vinca minor*. A high wrought-iron fence surrounds the site, with gates at each end; the central gate on the side leads to the middle terrace and its central feature. This is a colourful open pergola, in form reminiscent of two Greek temples impacted at right angles across each other to form a cross in plan. It is a deliberately jokey structure, set on diagonally laid brick pavers, the open steel lattice of rafters and beams hung with wisteria; tiny lights are inset above. The creampainted concrete columns are deliberate parodies of the Doric order, their entasis exaggerated to bulbousness. It is not a serious architectural essay,

(**Left**) Stairs lead up from the lower terrace to the pergola level, the transition edged with flowering plants.

(**Opposite**) Three sprays play from the brick paving of the lower terrace, a safe and legal updating of the children's tradition of turning on the fire hydrants in the streets of New York in hot weather. Here people can sit and watch the children play among the water or around the pergola a level up.

although it has resonances of some of the more exuberant designs of leading contemporary Post-Modern architects.

The vista from the side entrance is terminated by a blank screen wall, whose only feature is a lion's-head waterspout directed into a basin flanked by cherubim sitting on carved shells. It is a small, amusing decorative pleasure, perhaps redolent of European village plazas and the only small-scale referential joke to be found: minority neighbourhoods are suspicious of frivolous features.

Six steps lead up to the top terrace, which is planned very formally with fixed garden seats arranged on a wide brick path around a group of nine square flowerbeds. These are planted with spring bulbs, tulips, irises, day-lilies, daffodils and other brightly coloured plants, which the local people tend and replant themselves as part of the community deal. It is a quiet area for sitting out and pottering, an allusion to an old-world villa garden.

The lower terrace beyond the pergola is for children. Weintraub installed three spray jets mounted in the slightly concave brick paving, which is laid out in a pattern of concentric circles with a big diagonal square superimposed over them. The sprays are there to be watched and heard by people sitting on the park seats on either side and for children to play amongst. Traditionally, in hot weather children illegally turn on fire hydrants in the street and play, dangerously, among the spray. At Longfellow Garden the spray jets, a simple but dramatic device, are safe for children to play in; in less hot weather they serve the usual restful function of public fountains – but more interestingly because there is no restricting surrounding pool.

The park seats are arranged in a neutral row down either side of the terraces but on the middle terrace they can be easily shifted around to form socializing groups. The remainder, in the very satisfactory tradition of public park seating, neither encourage nor discourage people from talking to each other: not everybody goes to sit out in public spaces in the anticipation of socializing.

On the surface Longfellow Garden is a simple scheme with a playful piece of design rhetoric in the middle. Yet in one small space in this run-down urban setting it provides the local community, young and old, with a variety of possible uses, at once neutral and encouraging of play activities, a carefully tended oasis in the middle of urban blight.

2 PERCEPTIONS OF THE CULTURAL CONTEXT

In the new landscape one major theme is that of cultural context. It is based on the premise that environments are rather more than visual, that they inevitably have cultural and historical resonances. These may be indigenous, as at the Grupo de Diseño's Parque Tezozomoc in Mexico City, whose topography is deliberately designed as a reference to the pre-Hispanic topography of the Mexico Valley, or have exotic references, such as Bernard Lassus's Garden of Returns at Rochefort, once an important boat-building settlement, springboard for a thousand voyages to the undiscovered world and the home port for explorers and botanists returning their booty to the Old World. George Hargreaves's Plaza Park at San Jose makes reference to the history of settlement of the area. And in a different way the J. Paul Getty Museum garden, on its concrete raft above a valley at Malibu, provides an apt setting for the Greco-Roman collection housed within. At Sutton Place Sir Geoffrey Jellicoe has created a symbolic landscape whose ultimate references are to the Creation, while the Grand Mall Park in Yokohama is an extension of the cultural setting of the art museum.

Grand Mall Park, Yokohama, Japan.

2.1
Grupo de Diseño Urbano
PARQUE TEZOZOMOC
Azcapotzalco, Mexico City
1982
for Delegación Azcapotzalco, Departamento del Distrito Federal

(*Left*) The central lake, its edges alternately open and wooded.

This 30-hectare/75-acre recreational and cultural landscape is located in the middle of a polluted industrial zone of north-west Mexico City which is also densely packed with migrants. In so crowded an environment, public and recreational space is essential and the construction of the park was a matter of social urgency rather than simple civic pride. One of the goals set for the landscape architects Grupo de Diseño Urbano was the incorporation of some kind of reference to the vanished historical and cultural traces of the Valley of Mexico on which the modern city is founded.

The earliest mapped records of the area indicated that at least 12 pre-Hispanic settlements existed around the five contiguous lakes on which Mexico City was founded. This provided one starting-point for Grupo de Diseño Urbano's Mario Schjetnan: he took the early descriptions of the topography of the valley as a basis for his remodelling of the landscape, especially the area around the park's central lake. In a sense he created a giant topographical scale model. To underline the cultural heritage theme he worked with an historian, a biologist and a poet who researched the valley's history. They created texts which were mounted on black obelisks and set in small plazas, marking the position of the old settlements. They explain the myths and historical and environmental circumstances of the fifteenth-century settlements which they represent.

Parque Tezozomoc is of course more than that. It is a place for local people to promenade and cycle, watch outdoor performances or just sit. The most prominent feature of the big rectangular site is a lake, roughly in the formation of the original five Mexico Valley lakes. It is surrounded by heavy planting and, on one side, low hills created from the spoil of the excavations for the Mexico City rapid transit metro. The water for the lake and the park's irrigation is recycled from the drainage system of a nearby housing estate.

There are access points with small plazas and adjacent car-parking spaces all around the site, but the formal entrance is from the north-east and leads visitors down a long path to a great formal circular plaza with a jetting fountain in a round pool. It is a processional way of bringing the visitor into an otherwise non-linear organization of hills, winding paths and valleys, with only a few deliberately formal areas defining specific functions. One path leads south-east between an extensive rose garden on one side and an area for outdoor sculpture on the other. Another leads to a looping path through the plantation nursery and thence to the street. The very large nursery is not only for the park but for surrounding reforestation programmes.

Another path winds its way back north to children's play spaces and picnic areas or west around a small hill to the top end of the lake. On one side is an open-air auditorium with a hard-surfaced circular stage, overlooked by a circular look-out plaza on top of the highest new hill in the park. From it there are

(*Below*) The plan of Parque Tezozomoc is resonant of nineteenth-century European designs: curving paths among mounded topography encircling a lake. But the shape of the lake and its surrounding topography are based on those of the pre-Hispanic Mexico Valley. *Top left* are courts for ball games, *top right* children's play areas and *bottom right* the extensive nursery.

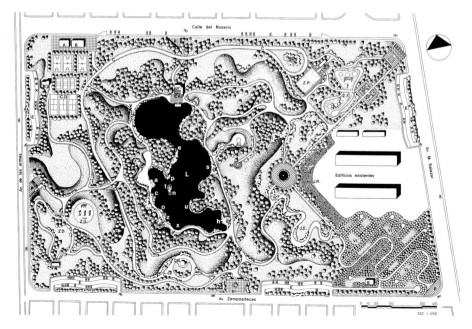

(*Right*) An inscribed black obelisk on the route around the lake represents the position of one of the pre-Hispanic settlements around the original Mexico Lake.

(*Left*) The serene lake with its perimeter walkway.

(*Left*) The central facility building, a cool essay in orthogonal architecture which complements the landscape detailing.

(*Above and opposite*) A sylvan setting not uninfluenced by the great nineteenth-century tradition of public park design, here with the underlying agenda of reference to the original formation of the Mexico Valley in pre-Hispanic times.

views across the lake with its island, representing the island of Tenochtitlan, the founding site of Mexico City, and north to the far distant mountains. To the north of the lake is a Modernist pavilion: it has reinforced concrete pilotis and an external stairway to the roof, and a pergolaed terrace with the bright blue cylinder of a water-tank rising through at one corner. It serves as a cafeteria and lavatories, and as a prospect platform for views down the length of the lake with its wooded promontories and inlets.

A bicycle path loops in a wide arc from a rental kiosk in a circular plantation round the western side of the lake to a looped termination to the north-east. It is separated from the strictly pedestrian paths, sometimes bridging over them, elsewhere swooping under them. In the north-west corner is a number of hard courts for ball games with adjacent maintenance and management facilities. South of these is a circular space for gymnastics. Near the main entrance is a skating court and children's playground.

The design of the park, with its winding paths, irregular lake and mounded topography, is reminiscent of mid-nineteenth-century public park plans by Paxton, Alphand and Olmsted; the obelisks and their texts are resonant of the didactic functions of botanical gardens of the same time — here, however, rather than introducing locals to the exotic flora of the wide world, their function is to introduce new settlers to the historical and cultural context of the territory to which they have been drawn. That is reinforced by the metaphor of the topography of the pre-Hispanic Mexico Valley. One of its important functions is therefore to create in a sense an abstraction which provides the visitor with the possibility of dissociating himself from the grim urban surroundings — another world.

2.2
Hargreaves Associates
San Jose Plaza Park
San Jose, California
1988
for San Jose Redevelopment Agency

George Hargreaves of Hargreaves Associates was commissioned by the city of San Jose to design a landscape for the city's oldest open space, a major focal point of the city both because it operates as a huge traffic island and because it is the centre of a number of important buildings – the art museum, a convention centre, a large hotel. The city wanted a significant public space where people could sit out, watch open-air events or stroll.

The site is a long rectangle with semicircular ends, and has a triangular traffic island at the west end. Hargreaves ran a wide path down the long east–west axis of the site and lined it with Victorian-style double lamp-standards and wooden seating. At the east end the path spreads out to form a narrow triangle of hard surface and then bifurcates to take pedestrians across the road to the north and south; here there is a platform for public performances.

Halfway along Hargreaves cut the site with a semicircular bank planted out with bright red flowers in season. The main path changes level here, down a set of stairs. On either side of these a semicircular gridded paved seating-area follows the bank's upper contour and the paving is continued in a quadrant formed by the bank's lower edge, the main axial path and a diagonal path across the plaza. Here 22 water jets are located at the intersections of the paving grid. They are programmed to start off as fog in the morning, gradually turning into low jets and at the end of the cycle into tall jets. At night the jets are lit from concealed lighting in the paving grid. The fountain area is self-draining so that adults and children using the park are able to move and play among the fountains rather than merely observing their changing patterns.

At first sight the remaining two paths running diagonally across the grassed plaza seem to be arbitrarily located. In fact they, like the main axial path, have been very carefully located along the paths that people naturally take between major buildings on either side of the public space.

(***Right***) **The centrepiece of the landscape from the south: a low banked crescent right across the site accommodating a change of level in the main east–west promenade, the quadrant to the south being the location of the gridded fountain. The basic paving grid also follows the upper perimeter of the crescent. Here the jets are slowly building height during the earlier part of the day.**

(***Below***) **Plan of Plaza Park with the quadrant fountain area (*centre*), the flowering orchard (*left*) and the performance area (*right*).**

The west section of the park is planted out with flowering fruit-trees arranged in a series of concentric segments focused on the main semicircular split in level. The path to the east and its triangular open space are surrounded by trees, which are also planted round much of the perimeter of the park. Like the main path, these paths are lit with Victorian-style double lamp-standards and lined with wooden seating.

All this is deceptively simple on plan: the ground-level experience is of people being able to cut across

(*Left*) The long axial walk running from west to east with deliberately traditional lamp standards and seating.

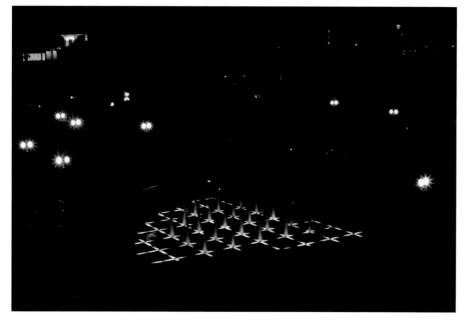

The fountain's water-jets are programmed to start off as mist in the early morning (*top left*) and gradually build up during the day (*middle left*) to their full height (*top right*). At night their sources are indicated by lighting set into the self-draining paving grid (*left, below*). Their changing height and spread changes the way people use the area: they walk easily through the mist or among the low jets, more circumspectly through or around the tall jets on windy days.

the park without walking on the grass, of making a promenade along its whole length, of browsing in weekend market stalls lining the path, watching street performers or playing among the fountains and, as in the best traditional parks, simply sitting and watching.

The design nevertheless contains a number of other references. Hargreaves argues that too much contemporary landscape is designed on the basis of arbitrary aesthetic considerations rather than deriving 'composition and meaning from the external world', that it is concerned with problem-solving rather than 'connecting people to the larger environment'. Thus Plaza Park's symbolic content is considerable. It is not the high symbolism of the unconscious but gentle references to the site and its history. For example, the grid of water jets makes reference to artesian wells bored near the site in the early 1800s, their growth over the day a kind of metaphor for the history of water which made the Santa Clara Valley flourish. The orchard is a reminder of the prolific interwar fruit-farms of the surrounding area, the deliberately old-fashioned lamp-standards are a reference to the 300-year-old history of the city and, it has been argued, the night-time illuminated fountain grid refers to the high technology of contemporary Silicon Valley.

It is not as if these elements are either immediately obvious or yet part of a secret Post-Modern agenda capable of being read only by other designers. What is evident, however, is that they and the organization of the routes through the park are based on simple referential or commonsense premises which Hargreaves has synthesized into a major piece of public landscape.

(**Above**) The view east towards the flowering orchard. The cross path follows existing pedestrian 'desire lines' from buildings on the streets either side of the park.

2.3
Sir Geoffrey Jellicoe
SUTTON PLACE
Surrey, UK
1982
for Stanley Seeger

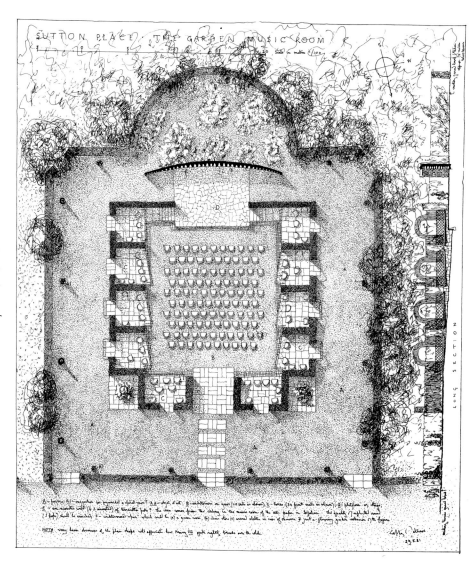

Sir Geoffrey Jellicoe was asked by the wealthy collector Stanley Seeger to design a new landscape for the sixteenth-century Sutton Place, which Seeger had begun to refurbish following his purchase of it after the death of J. Paul Getty. In the tradition of great eighteenth- and nineteenth-century estate designs, it was to combine close-grained textures around the house with a broader sweep beyond.

Sutton Place had been laid out by Richard Weston in 1525. Little of the original landscape remained, or of the work done on it by Capability Brown and, more recently, Gertrude Jekyll. The U-shaped house faced north, with a services court to the west. A long axis ran from the main approach avenue through the main entrance court and through the centre of the house.

The thrust of Jellicoe's design was to create walled gardens on either side of the house, with a long straight walk running along their southern boundary and the south wall of the house. Beyond that a lawn led down to the woods to the south; incorporated in its slopes was to be a cascade. To the north of the house Jellicoe created a lake, visible from the house and from the approach road.

The design is in many ways influenced by Italian Mannerist gardens which, Jellicoe has argued, represent the first time that 'the garden as an idea broke free of the academic rules, to become companion rather than handmaiden to the house'. He sees the landscape as a continuum of past, present and future, and in that sense his is a continuation and development of what already existed in terms of axes, vistas and the probable intentions of the original designer.

As in Italian Renaissance and Mannerist gardens, much of the detailed design is made up of discrete elements. The gardens around the house are essentially rooms. They are to the east and west; a walled garden with a formal pool behind the service yard leads into a larger kitchen garden laid out as parterres with a small orchard of trees in quincunx formation.

To the east, french doors from the house lead directly out to stepping-stones set in a long pool, the moat, and across into the Paradise Garden, a semi-

(*Above*) Jellicoe's design for an open-air theatre, in which the 'boxes' on either side of the main auditorium were to be formed in vaulted hedging with stone floors and the whole surrounded by an apsed rectangle of hedges. Around the 'auditorium' the lawn served as an open-air foyer for guests at Stanley Seeger's music events.

(*Above*) A new folly built into part of the new wall surrounding the gardens adjacent to the house.

(*Opposite, below*) Jellicoe's original plan for the garden: in the middle is the U-shaped house with a courtyard and service wing to the left. The Paradise Garden is immediately to the right of the house and beyond it the Moss or Secret Garden. To the far left are two kitchen gardens. The Long Walk runs from left to right immediately below the walled complex of house and gardens, with dark pergolas at intervals. Below the Long Walk is a sloping green and, on the main axis of the middle of the house, a cascade, commencing with formal square pools and, as the water enters the wood, gradually becoming freer in form. To the left is the open-air theatre and above it the Ben Nicholson sculpture and its pool. Some of the elements were not built and some were moved.

formal garden set with bowers and trellises for climbing plants. A hedge separates this from the Moss Garden, the 'secret garden', an enclosed, apparently natural area which is actually based on two intersecting circles, one of moss and one of lawn. A cobbled serpentine path leads around the garden to a gazebo set at one corner of the brick walls which enclose both gardens.

Adjacent to the great wall running east–west to the south of the house, some of it old and some newly built in matching bricks, is the Long Walk. Sections

(*Left*) The moat outside the library doors is crossed by stepping-stones. Beyond is the great wall on the other side of which is the Long Walk.

(*Above*) The semi-formal Paradise Garden, with bowers for climbing roses and brick-paved paths. Behind is the enclosing wall shared by the Secret Garden.

of this are covered by pergolas, creating dark and faintly mysterious tunnels of foliage leading to an existing pool and a vast white marble geometric sculpture by the English artist Ben Nicholson. Part of the Long Walk overlooks a sloping lawn and then a gentle slope which provides the right topography for the cascade. Off to one side is a projected Music Room, an open-air amphitheatre with movable 'stall' seating and surrounding 'boxes' defined by yew hedges. The whole was to be surrounded by a hedge in the form of an apse-ended square. The cascade was designed to start at its high point on the main central axis of the house with a set of rectangular pools. As the cascade moved down into the wood to the south, the pools became increasingly elongated and arbitrary in shape, hidden eventually by the trees.

The design is not a Mannerist pastiche, however. Jellicoe's underlying purpose was to create an allegory – less the direct Aenean allegory of, say, Stourhead, but rather more that of man's place in the cosmos, 'a grand allegory of creation, life and aspiration . . . links and ideas which reflect a lighter or darker mood of the subconscious'. The lake is therefore in the shape of a fish, which has both the banal connotation of water and a more esoteric mystical one, its surrounding hills deliberately composed to represent, as Jellicoe describes it, 'the man-woman-child complex . . . immemorial in art'.

The Long Walk from the east, with deliberately out-of-scale urns, the hanging wood to the right and, before the house in the background, a pergola. The final view down this walk was intended to be mysterious and somewhat Magritte-esque.

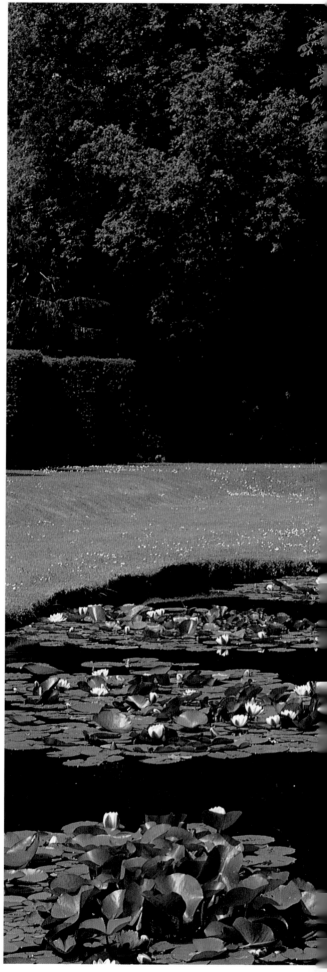

The Long Walk's gently mysterious passages are references to Magritte, in the sense of juxtaposing unexpected and unfamiliar elements with each other. The Moss Garden, with its interconnecting circles (which have since disappeared) of moss and lawn centred on two large trees, has a secret significance – as does the passage from the ground floor of the library across stepping-stones to the bowers and pergolas of the Paradise Garden. Here the significance is the 'difficulty' with which the owner of the house has to contend in order to gain access to the 'paradise' on the other side of the moat.

These are gentle references to other things outside the day-to-day world, rather perhaps than allegories, but it is unusual for this kind of consideration to form the basis for a contemporary landscape design.

Not all of Jellicoe's design was built by the time Seeger sold the property, and it is doubtful if many major features such as the cascade will ever be built.

(*Above*) Natural woodland and a classicizing sculpture by the Long Walk.

(*Right*) The Ben Nicholson sculpture, embodying geometric elements significant in the allegory of the whole garden, is enclosed by its sheltering hedge, repeated in the reflecting pool in front.

2.4
Bernard Lassus

LE PARC DE LA CORDERIE ROYALE

Rochefort-sur-Mer, France
1988

for the City of Rochefort

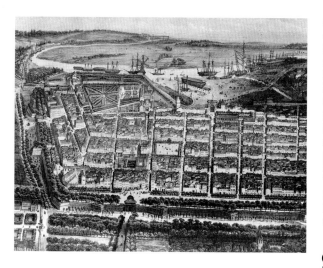

In 1982 the French landscape theorist and designer Bernard Lassus won a national competition to create a landscape around the restored Corderie Royale de Rochefort, the immensely long, low, narrow building running north–south parallel with the Charente river, originally designed as a rope factory for Louis XIV's navy. The town of Rochefort had been developed by Colbert as a naval arsenal on the Charente, strategically located several miles inland out of sight of the Atlantic. It became the seaport from which most French explorers, merchants, botanists and indeed armies departed for the New World.

Adjacent to the corderie were several docks and dry docks for building new ships and behind it a large open space, the Terrace Bégon, at a higher level behind the retaining walls of the town. An early *intendant*, Michel Bégon, had given his name to the begonia; his grandson, R.M. de La Galissonière, brought back the first seeds of the large-flowered magnolia which now bears his name. These and many other exotic plants brought back from the New World formed the basis for an extensive acclimatizing garden behind the corderie.

In 1926 the arsenal was closed down, in 1945 the corderie was burned by the Germans and by the early 1970s the derelict ruins were invisible behind the overgrown river-front. The town started restoring the old building in 1974 and later, with the support of President Mitterand, called the competition.

(*Below*) The outline of Lassus's scheme around the restored Corderie building. Vistas are cut through the original dense undergrowth and foliage lining the river (*right, top right*); the parallel town wall above the Corderie has been restored, and a long ramp descends in front of it from the broad terrace above to a single line of palm trees leading to the conservatories. The old dry docks to the far left are now used for the display of maritime artefacts.

(*Right*) The aerial view shows the site of the Corderie when Lassus was asked to start work.

(*Overleaf*) The view from the eastern end of the old town wall with the restored Corderie (*right*) and the great ramp with its trees leading to the palm-tree-lined walk towards the conservatories (*out of frame on the right*).

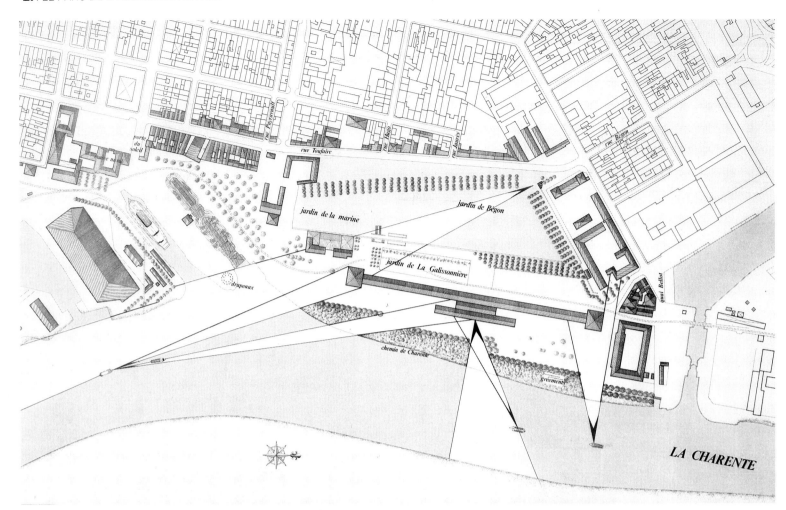

jardin de la marine

jardin de Bégon

jardin de La Galissonnière

drapeaux

chemin de Charente

gréements

quai Bellot

LA CHARENTE

Lassus was concerned first of all about the relationship of the corderie and the river – and by implication the sea. By opening up three large gaps in the vegetation which had grown up along the river-bank he re-established the old relationship: as a riverside building with a former sea arsenal town above and behind it. On an old concrete block he established the Rigging Area, where replicas of the masts and rigging made in the building formed the basis of a children's play area. Near the masts are displays of exotic outdoor plants in wicker baskets, referring to the botanical specimens which had been brought back to the corderie since the seventeenth century.

In addition, to reinforce the riverside walk in front of the corderie he planted reeds, willows, alders and ash along the river-bank, with carefully pruned trees along what is now a meadow. The corderie is the home for a number of organizations and a local public library.

The two dry docks to the south of the corderie were cleaned out and used as the real dry docks for building replica ships, based on plans in Diderot's *Encyclopédie*. At the south entrance of the dry docks is a ring of flagpoles bearing the pennants of the various admirals of the arsenal, and at the other a labyrinth, the Labyrinth of Naval Battles. Here, among a heavy

green clipped mass of hedge plants with paths in blue gravel, visitors are intended to don helmets and control boxes and re-enact computerized historic naval battles as they move through the maze.

Establishing a renewed relationship with the town (called for by the competition) presented other problems. One obvious possibility was to create an avenue leading from the town to the centrepoint of the corderie. But, argued Lassus, this had never been a monumental building but an industrial structure. His solution was to create a great ramp running down outside the town wall from the north end of the Terrace Bégon to the rear of the corderie. It is planted with tulip trees originally brought back from Virginia and leads on to a row of palm trees.

(*Above*) Lassus's schematic plan showing the views newly available both from the river and from the site out to the river and the surrounding countryside.

(*Left*) The single row of palms continuing the line of the great ramp.

(*Opposite*) The great ramp, with the upper terrace to the right behind the old town wall.

(*Above*) Evocations of the cultural context: on either side the original seventeenth-century constructions; between them reminders of the great exotic horticultural function of this disembarkation point from the New World.

There is a deliberately unexpected juxtaposition of the classical architecture of the corderie and these unusual, exotic plantings culled from the corners of the earth. As Lassus puts it, 'we feel the surprise the navigators of old must have felt when they saw them for the very first time'.

At the south end of this Bégon Garden is a collection of glasshouses containing the collection purchased by the town, the nationally famous Millerioux begonia collection, plants provided by the Brazilian landscape architect Roberto Burle Marx and, in an orangery, specimens of the plants brought back by Admiral de La Galissonière in the early eighteenth century. In the tradition of the age the plants are brought outdoors in their tubs during the spring and summer.

Lassus maintains that meaning cannot be reinvented from outside and that it is the deep cultural roots which landscape must address. At Rochefort it was simply a matter of clearing the ground 'in order to disclose the depth which existed at the surface . . . reinvent it once again.'

The National Trust

restoration of

CLAREMONT

Surrey, UK
1975–81
for the National Trust

From round 1717 Charles Bridgeman had worked with Sir John Vanbrugh on the improvements to the estate which Vanbrugh had sold to the Duke of Newcastle in Surrey. Vanbrugh had designed a castellated belvedere, one of the first medievalizing follies, on a hilltop behind the house. It was offset from the main axis of the house and the parterres and avenues which Bridgeman designed for the front.

The woodland-covered hill had winding paths and vistas, and to the west of the belvedere Bridgeman laid out a round pond with a grass amphitheatre on one side. The amphitheatre is a curious formation in plan: it consists of two unequal semicircles with a common centre point, the larger stepped up from a central circular platform at an intermediate level and the smaller stepped down. The two are separated by a wall of earth forming ramps up either side of the central platform to the height of the upper curved terraces, where there are additional banked earth buttresses.

In the 1730s William Kent worked on softening Bridgeman's lines, changing the circular pool to a more irregular shape with a sylvan island in the middle; he added a small temple and a grotto on the shore. Bridgeman had designed a short formal avenue on axis with the house and its parterre, with another avenue at right angles across the pleasure grounds in front of the house, terminating on the east with a circular pond surrounded by trees. There were other formal geometric features around the Bridgeman landscape including a kitchen garden, pools, prospect points and a bowling green. Kent substituted a lawn for the parterre and replaced the main avenue with scattered trees. By breaking up the geometric lines he softened and naturalized Bridgeman's work. At the back of the house, to the east of the wooded hill and the belvedere, Bridgeman had set out a pleasure ground scattered with trees. Kent extended the ha-ha dividing the designed landscape from the meadow and made it more naturalistic.

An early-eighteenth-century view of the lake and amphitheatre at Claremont, a schematically correct view but entirely misrepresenting the scale of this part of the landscape: a leisurely walk around the lake takes about 20 minutes. The photographs on the following pages provide a better idea. The amphitheatre was specially constructed: it is effectively a carefully sculptured mound with trees planted up its crest to suggest hanging woods behind.

Subsequent gardeners had worked at Claremont, and by the time the National Trust had acquired the property in 1949 the landscape had deteriorated almost beyond recognition.

The major problem faced by contemporary landscape preservationists is to which design a landscape should be restored. That is partly affected by the availability of good documentary information and by the problem of whether contemporary illustrators could be entirely relied upon to depict accurately what they saw, rather than what the owner wanted to see. There is also a natural reluctance to root out mature existing planting in the name of historical accuracy. This is especially true when information about the fine detail of original gardens is inevitably sketchy and when subsequent planting makes a brave show for the paying public who visit National Trust properties. Eighteenth-century planting was (to modern eyes) relatively sparse, with fewer flowers and less colour.

At Claremont the decision was made to work to the model of the Kent design. Its contours were still just visible, and reverting to the Bridgeman layout would have called for massive earth-moving and a long wait until the avenues and formal features had matured.

The task of restoring Claremont was carried out by the National Trust's agent, Peter Mansfield, with the help of the Trust's specialist advisers. Working with the estate's professional gardeners and a large number of student volunteers, he cleared the property of obviously alien growth and dead and diseased trees, including those destroyed by the 1987 gales. He planted mature oak and beech, sweet chestnut and limes. The main eighteenth-century planting had been essentially a variety of shades of green and of round-topped hardwoods together with some rhododendron and laurel. To the existing daffodils and wild flowers in the meadow to the north-east the Trust added bluebells, azaleas and viburnum and much of the grass was resown. The ph of the soil was very low – around 5.6 – so the whole area had to be covered by chalk to build up the alkaline content.

Kent's ha-ha north of the house between the pleasure grounds and the meadow had been turf, altered later to brick to provide a sharper edge. It had become a ditch and extensive work was carried out to refurbish the original profile. The wooded hill behind the house was replanted and its meandering paths and the formal approach to the belvedere restored.

View from one of the bastions at the side of the amphitheatre down and across the lake.

The most unusual feature of the landscape remained the amphitheatre to the north-west. Its lake, originally lined with puddled clay, was dredged for silt and its edges were smartened up. The amphitheatre, which was barely recognizable, was regraded with mechanical equipment by skilful operators. The semicircular mound had been sown relatively recently with Indian cedars. The original design probably had beeches in this position. But, as elsewhere in the restoration, a judgement had to be made and the cedars remained.

As with any landscape restoration which is to be opened to the public, Claremont represents a pragmatic compromise between probable historical accuracy, available funds and the need to create the essential spirit of a great eighteenth-century landscape.

(*Top, above*) The folly, designed by Vanbrugh, at the top of the ridge behind the house; the pictures show it before and after restoration.

(*Right*) The great amphitheatre from across the lake. Its function is more to do with demonstrations of three-dimensional classical geometry and resonances of the classical past than with re-creating a classical Greek theatre.

2.6
Tokyo Landscape Architects
GRAND MALL PARK
Nishi-ku, Yokohama City, Japan
1989
for the City of Yokohama

Tokyo Landscape Architects were asked to design a significant landscape space across the front of Yokohama's city art museum. Their brief was to design a space which was integrated with the museum and its surroundings, which could be used for public and cultural events and which could also be used by the people of the city as a park, somewhat in the new tradition of city-centre pocket parks.

The designers, under the project management of Haruto Kobayashi and the concept planner Tatsushi Yamanaka, took the view that the landscape should have four major underlying arguments. One was to do with the idea of the space as symbol, another to do with directness in the creation of clearly designed elements, a third with the concept of space as theatre both metaphorically and practically, and the fourth with the idea of the park in the town, the landscape as street corner.

The 1.2-hectare/3-acre site is aligned with the axis of a linear park running north–south and its middle point is on the axis of the art museum. The designers believed that the strong axiality of the setting called for a more or less symmetrical layout. That has

(*Below*) **Plan: the art museum along the bottom, fronted with two fountain pools either side of the raised 'stage'. The two *yakokai* are in front of each pool, either side of the central square pavement. The pair of groves beyond completes the raised middle section. Terraces, ramps and stairs provide the transition either side to street level.**

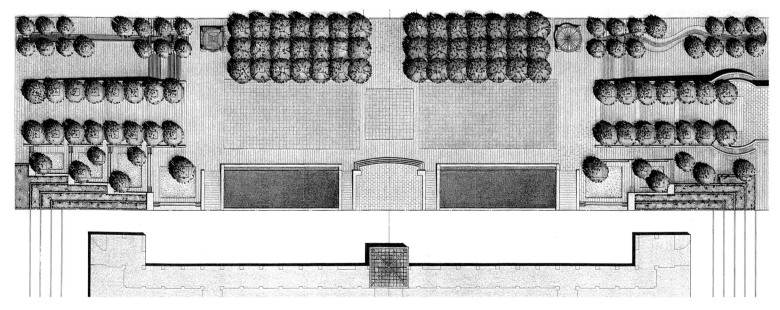

(Above) The change of level from the raised zones in front of the museum is achieved on the left by a long ramp and on the right by terracing, each level with its own keynote tree.

meant a division into 12 sections on plan of roughly equal size, organized as three lateral zones running north–south crossed by four transverse east–west zones. The two middle of these zones, mirror images of each other, are built up to the same level as the museum entrance, 3 metres/10 ft above the adjacent ground levels. The change of level from here to either edge of the site is achieved by respectively terracing, sloping and stepping the outer three transverse zones on each side. Almost the whole area is paved in dark stone, with trees planted directly into the pavement, many of them associated with elegant timber and stone benches.

The lateral zone nearest the museum has a low stage area on axis with its entrance, and a rectangular basin on either side lined with water-jets canted inwards to form a water shape somewhat reminis-cent of Renaissance water shows. Beyond the fountains at each end the ground is terraced down in four platforms to street level. The area in front of the museum marking the crossing of the two axes has been raised, partly to relate to the level of the entrance and more importantly to make it clear to visitors that this is an artificial ensemble, an urban space which has been deliberately created for them.

The second lateral zone has a central area (crossing the two middle transverse zones); rectangular areas on either side have sloping ground between rows of liquidambar trees. The south slope is terminated with a circular formation. The designers have des-cribed the two areas either side of the central plaza as *yakokai*, a word meaning literally 'night shining sea', and in addition to the reflective paint they have light-fittings built into the pavement.

(*Left*) View from the grove across the open paved area to the façade of the museum with quiescent water-jets and illuminated areas lit from under the elegant seats.

(*Above*) The *yakokai*, 'night shining sea', serves as a foreground to the billowing jets fronting the museum.

The middle sections of the third zone have *Zelkova serrata* trees planted formally in three rows, with open domed trellises at each end and wide stairs leading down to paved plazas at each side. The stairs also act as cascades for tree-lined streams, the north one running in a straight formal channel, the south stream meandering along a bed formed by the slope of the paving.

These three lateral zones, water, pavement painted with reflective paint and the corridor of trees, have a symbolic function. They represent respectively water, light and greenness. In functional terms they represent a zone where events happen, water, performances and the like, a zone where people gather and walk and a corridor zone with a series of carefully designed formal naturalistic elements, streams, two groves of trees and *treillages*.

The basic rules of planting have been to locate evergreens in the middle with deciduous trees around the perimeter of the site in order to achieve a comfortable transition from the surrounding area. Each section of the landscape has specific trees with one or more 'symbol trees'. For example, in the north-east plaza on the ocean side of the site are malus and *Ilex pedunculosa* diagonally opposite each other across the stream. Ground planting generally is *Rhododendron indicum*. Other trees include *Cornus florida* in the two outer sections of the south lateral zone, magnolia and *Ilex rotunda*.

(*Top*) The formality of the water-jets complements the formality of the museum façade, the open domed pergolas at each end of the grove the Post-Modern entrance canopy to the museum.

(*Above*) The stream meandering through the paved lower piazza cascades down the flight of stairs, with the *treillage* marking the end of the grove on the level above.

Emmet L. Wemple

J. PAUL GETTY
MUSEUM
Malibu, California
1974

for J. Paul Getty

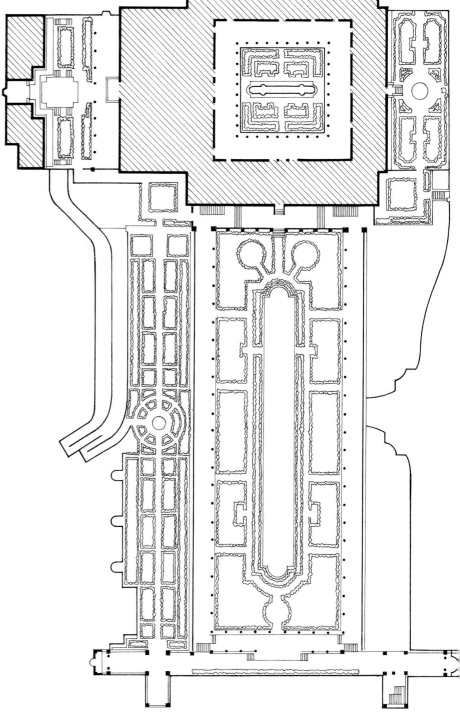

The design of the J. Paul Getty Museum is based on the Villa dei Papiri, discovered in the mid-eighteenth century under the volcanic rock at Herculaneum on the Bay of Naples. Emmet Wemple's task was faithfully to capture the spirit of the original villa's landscaping. Southern California's climate is similar to that of the Bay of Naples, so there was a good possibility that the plants thought to have been used at the Villa dei Papiri would thrive at Malibu. There was no hard evidence about precisely which plants were used, but there was enough generalized knowledge available about contemporary Roman landscape preferences and planting, some of it based on analysis of carbonized seeds, fruit and other plant material from Herculaneum, and some on descriptions in the writings of the two Plinys.

Advised by the historian-archaeologist Norman Neuerburg, the project landscape architect, Denis L. Kurutz, and the architects, Langdon and Wilson, worked closely together on this quintessentially architectural landscape. In fact the villa housing the museum and the set-pieces are set on a concrete raft above the steeply sloping 10-hectare/25-acre site, with car parking underneath. Visitors are encouraged to climb the stairs at the seaward end of the car park, to emerge under an open loggia at the end of the main peristyle garden. At the end of the long pool and its surrounding parterres is the front of the house. Looking back from the loggia is a view of the Pacific – both a reference to the original villa's seaside location and perhaps a reassurance that this is still twentieth-century California.

The main peristyle garden is surrounded by a Tuscan colonnade on three sides and a Corinthian loggia fronting the two-storey house which holds the main collection. The low marble surround to the long pool is edged with ivy trained over spherical wire armatures. The perimeter path is gravelled and surrounded by the Roman forerunners of parterres: low box hedges defining simple geometric shapes, within which are planted a variety of flowers includ-

ing roses, oleanders, alyssum, violets, irises, and woolly yarrow. Shrubs used in these locations include myrtle and butcher's broom. At the edge of the garden a row of trimmed laurel trees runs down each side in front of the east and west colonnades. Two arbours near the house are covered with trailing vines and trellises at the other end are planted with acanthus. Here and there in this formal symmetrical layout are fan palms and pomegranate trees.

The slab supporting the villa is designed to take loads of up to 60 cm/2 ft of soil. That was not sufficient for trees to grow in, and cylindrical 'wells'

(*Above*) **Plan of the museum and its landscape.**

(*Right*) The seaward end
of the main peristyle,
overlooking the Pacific
to the left and
surrounded by the
hanging woods of the
local Malibu hills.

extending 120 cm/4 ft below slab level had to be incorporated to give roots a sufficient hold. Before all the soil was placed an extensive irrigation system was installed to feed and water plant material unobtrusively: sprinklers would have been out of character.

The axis of the main peristyle garden passes into the house, through the entrance vestibule to the square inner peristyle garden around which the house is built. Its transverse axis leads on one side to the east garden and on the other, through a loggia, to the west garden. As in Roman gardens, evergreen plants predominate: laurel, box, myrtle, ivy and oleander. Bulbs and seeds were imported from Italy and acclimatized in California before being re-planted. Wemple's colour palette is predominantly green, with seasonal colours provided by annuals.

The fourth landscape element is the herb garden, which runs parallel with the main peristyle garden on the other side of its colonnaded west wall. This is a re-creation of a Roman kitchen garden, planted out with herbs, vegetables and fruit: mint, dill, thyme, camomile; garlic, peas; apple, peach, fig and citrus

(**Above**) The herb garden outside the main west wall of the peristyle garden is laid out as a series of formal squares, each with its own kitchen plant species.

(**Right**) Through the open peristyle to the south: the main peristyle garden and its pool are surrounded by colonnades and closed off by the façade of the main museum building, a self-contained ensemble which recreates the form of the original Villa dei Papiri at Herculaneum.

trees; and grapevines. They have been changed as more knowledge has been gained of ancient planting practice. This is a long linear garden with a central path, the middle marked by a ronde and terminated at the seaward side by an open portico. Planting is in slightly raised rectangular beds on either side. The plain outer wall of the peristyle on the east is reflected on the west by stone-walled terraces planted with olives, backed by the varied natural planting of the ridge behind.

At the north end by the house a path leads to the terraced west garden, planted with ivy, broom and yew. The upper terrace is backed by the museum's tea rooms. The centrepiece is a square pool at ground level, framed by stairs mounting the rise to the upper terrace. Its retaining wall is hung with ivy; box hedges enclose annuals. Open pergolas are hung with vines and sweet bays in pots stand in front of the twisted columns of the deep veranda facing the garden.

The east garden on the other side of the house terminates the main east–west cross axis which runs through the house, picking up its atrium, the pool of the inner peristyle garden and the circular pool of the

east garden. This garden is the same size but on a single level, with the low walls of the big fountain basin edged with butcher's broom; London plane trees are the major large-scale planting. The garden is surrounded by a stuccoed wall, beyond which heavy planting gives the impression of hanging woods.

The inner peristyle garden's main feature is a long pool on whose white marble edge stand five guardian bronze statues of women, with a border of ivy and more ivy on spherical wire armatures. The parterres are edged with low box hedges enclosing topiary shrubs: myrtle and butcher's broom. As elsewhere, gravel forms the main ground surface.

The fact that the villa is a pastiche of a building from another country and age has attracted a great deal of criticism from the design world. But that has not prevented visitors from coming to the museum and its gardens in large numbers. It is probable that the relative rigidity of the landscape strategy and planting is stiffer than was the case in ancient Herculaneum, but then the final function of this landscape is perhaps most to do with education – a variation on the tradition of botanical landscape design and unique on this scale in the modern world.

(*Above*) **The east garden, with its central pool, uses surrounding trees beyond the enclosing wall to form a more natural background than elsewhere in the museum's landscape ensembles.**

(*Right*) **The gravelled inner peristyle garden, enclosed on four sides, is a recreation of one of the models for the Renaissance parterre. The spherical plants are ivy on wire armatures.**

3 THE STRUCTURED LANDSCAPE

The new landscape eschews the conventional landscape wisdoms of the past hundred or so years, which in most cases is heavily orientated to a form of naturalism. Dan Kiley has for a long time designed on the basis of a formal organization of his landscape, classic in the sense that its foundations include the traditions of both Islam and the West. His are ordered landscapes, normally with a clear geometric plan structure which nevertheless reads excitingly in three dimensions. The Deconstructivist Bernard Tschumi on the other hand deliberately abandons formal order. At La Villette he has devised three separate ordering systems and then wilfully arranged them over each other without any registration. At the Rio Shopping Center, Atlanta, Georgia, Martha Schwartz explains the process in more graphic language as having collected the various elements of the design, thrown them up and left them to lie where they fell. Dani Freixes with Vicente Miranda at the Parque del Clot, Barcelona, and Alexandre Chemetoff in his Bamboo Garden at La Villette have operated with similar layering processes, deploying existing sections of the site's archaeology as 'found' ordering systems whose physical appearance has then been altered in an ironic way.

The Bamboo Garden in the Parc de la Villette, Paris.

3.1
Martha Schwartz (The Office of Peter Walker/Martha Schwartz)
RIO SHOPPING CENTER
Atlanta, Georgia
1988
for Ackerman & Company

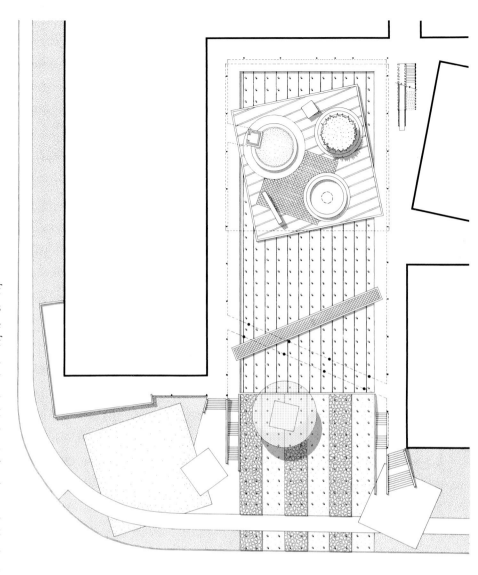

Working with the architect Bernardo Fort Brescia of Arquitectonica, Martha Schwartz designed this landscape to enhance a speciality commercial centre in mid-town Atlanta. Built in an area in need of revitalizing, the U-shaped shopping building is on two levels, the ground floor 3 metres/10 ft below street level. The rear third of the large court is roofed over, creating a double-height open space for eating and food concessions. The front third ramps up to street level with public access stairs on either side. A diagonal bridge connects the two wings of the upper level and a path at pavement level crosses the pool which forms the centre section of the court.

Schwartz poised a 12-metre/40-ft tubular steel geodesic sphere halfway down the slope. It has a mist fountain in its base, surrounded by ferns, and is draped with green vines. From the street it acts as a striking signpost for the shopping centre; from within it serves both as a focus and a partial closure for the open street end of the court. The slope connecting street and court is laid out with alternating strips of grass and painted rock fragments. Over this and across the pool is laid a grid of gilded frogs. They all face the sphere – as if in worship. In the pool they are mounted on pedestals so that they appear to be sitting on the water surface. The pool is painted black, with white parallel lines running longitudinally rather like swimming lanes in conventional training pools. They are actually fibre-optic strips which glow under the water at night. A white, black-banded path runs diagonally across the pool and the bright red overhead walkway, skewed in the opposite direction, is supported by deliberately heavy black columns with spiral fluting, rather like tightly twisted liquorice sticks.

Under the high canopy the plaza is set at a skew to the rectangle of the pool. It reads as a floating square which has broken its moorings and swung out of its original position at the end of the court. Its floor is patterned with squares and circles, one containing plants, another a circular bar and yet another a small

grove of 15-metre/50-ft bamboos which rise through a circular cut-out in the roof. The plaza is the primary meeting-place for the scheme. It also contains a lift shaft with a video wall display by the artist Darra Birnbaum.

The brief was to create a vibrant space with a high level of visibility, excitement and activity which would draw attention into the court from the road and achieve the transition between the differing levels of street and court. At the same time it had to create a memorable image among the busy clutter of the street environment outside. Schwartz's aim was to create a wild, pop, loud ambience using bold, intense colours: reds, blues, blacks, yellows and greens. Somewhat Constructivist in design, it has been composed as a series of individual forms which have fallen into seemingly arbitrary positions overlaying each other. The striations in the black pool floor read as a primary ordering geometry, but they change with the banding of the front slope. The two cross routes connecting either arm of the shopping building are set at different slants, the striations of the plaza floor are shifted round so as not to align with its edges and a small chequerboard square is laid over

(*Above*) **The Rio Shopping Center plan: at first-floor level (slightly higher than street level) a U-shaped building has a diagonal walkway connecting the two wings (dotted) and roofed over the upper third. At ground level the ground slopes down to the rectangular pool with the open sphere at the bottom. The pool is crossed by a low-level walkway and in its upper third has the square public platform apparently dropped at a skew across it: an ensemble of dislocated geometries.**

(*Above*) The sphere rests in a square bed of ferns skewed slightly across the banded pattern of the slope, with a mist fountain at the bottom. It is there that the gilded frogs' orientation to the sphere is most obvious.

(*Right*) Apparently sitting on the surface of the pool, the frogs, from a local hardware store, provide a constant grid for the scheme. They are located on a grid defined by longitudinal fibre-optic lines in the pool floor.

this at yet another angle, with the circles laid on top of this. Finally, the grid of the gilded plaster frogs serves as another layer, parallel with but otherwise unrelated to the ordering patterns and the pool and slope underneath. It is a composition of overlapping and rotated squares of lawn, paving and stones, over which are laid other geometries such as lines, circles, spheres and cubes, all set in the context of a mysterious black luminously striated pool.

But in addition to the dislocated geometries the design incorporates deliberate enigmas. The plaza roof has two circular cut-outs: one for the tall bamboo and the other apparently for nothing, although it may be to allow natural rainfall watering for the circular planting bed almost below.

The relentless grid of frogs is an historical resonance from the Bassin de Latone at Versailles. In ordinary circumstances banal plaster garden ornaments, here they are given a kind of ironic meaning by being painted gold and arranged in their mysterious black pool and up the slope, all facing the mist-wreathed latticed orb which seems set to roll into the pool at any moment.

Schwartz has created more than a loud, pop, delightful visual environment. It is one that sets the viewer aback once he has taken his first glance and induces one of the old traditional experiences of landscape: uncertainty.

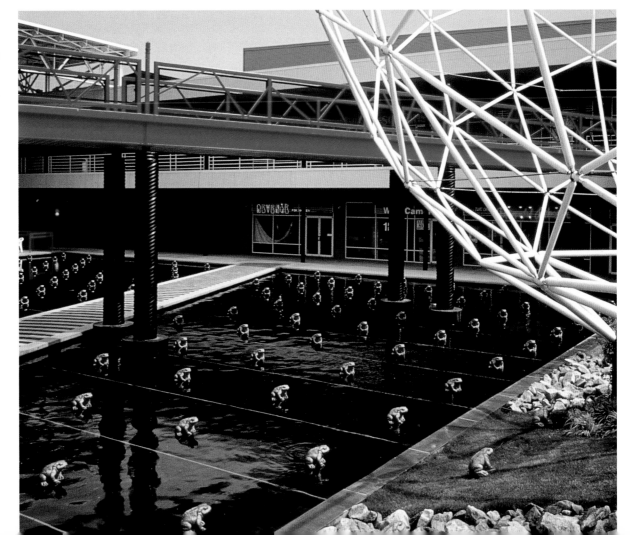

(*Right*) **The relentless and faintly sinister grid of gilded frogs provides a kind of ordering matrix across which walkways at two levels skew from one side of the shopping centre to the other. Behind is a relatively banal commercial shopping development building.**

(*Opposite*) **The roofed public entertainment platform, with its deliberately dislocated paving patterns and the three big circles with an audio-visual column at one side.**

3.2
Dani Freixes and Vicente Miranda

PARQUE DEL CLOT
Barcelona
1986
for Barcelona Council

In the mid-1980s the city of Barcelona started an active programme of creating public parks, plazas and other public facilities. Dani Freixes, working with Vicente Miranda, designed the Parque del Clot on a former industrial railway site in the eastern section of the city. They established a number of preliminary criteria. It was important that enough of the existing railway building structure should remain to maintain a continuity with the site's cultural past, although not necessarily without modification. They also saw that the planning had to accommodate different uses which might in some cases be reversible. A concomitant of that was not particularly specifying any part of the park's functions. Another was the need to concentrate the building work in order to permit more woodland and to create a focus on the main plaza, the heart of the project.

Their design divides the site roughly into two. On the north is a mounded semi-naturalistic landscape, on the south a main plaza, paved and sunk seven or eight feet below ground level with a raised paved podium across the south side reached by a wide flight of stairs. A skewed bridge connects the podium with a wooded hill to the north-east and a long bridge links the western boundary with the centre of the hilly section.

Freixes and Miranda kept much of the old arched factory wall standing around the site; it now reads as a freestanding arcade around the west, north and east sides. On the west the middle section of the old wall has been set in a shallow waterway with bubbling fountains and a sandy beach leading up to the main mound. Ambiguously, the pool has been set halfway down the wide flight of stairs leading from street level to the sunken plaza. The top of the wall which stands in the pool has been transformed from an arched arcade into an aqueduct, spilling water down the old brickwork into the pool.

Near the south end of the 'aqueduct' another walkway emerges from between the arches at high

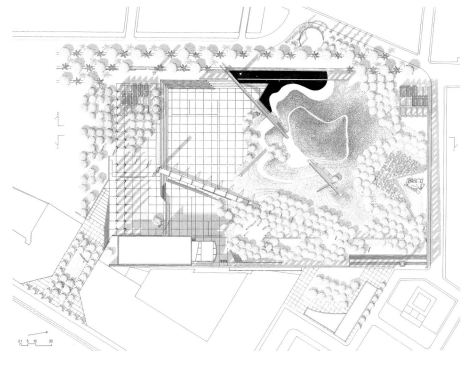

(*Opposite, below*) Plan of the Parque del Clot: north is to the right. The entrance plaza (*bottom right*) leads through the fragments of the arched openings of the old building and up the broad stairs to the wooded mound. The two footways lead left to the raised plaza and up to the northern entrance through the 'aqueduct' and thence to the street. A secondary entrance plaza to the left provides an approach to the raised plaza on the left. Here is an apparently arbitrary layering of ordering systems whose inner logic actually relates to pedestrian desire lines across the site.

(*Left*) Outside, the old walls are transformed into an aqueduct set in a linear pool, with one of the illuminated beacons signposting the park. The stairway up to the long walkway over the sunken plaza is behind.

(*Below*) The enclosure for the western entrance stairs simply impacts into the old wall, in a frank acceptance of old and new.

level, crosses the sunken plaza area at a skew, simply impacts into the side of the hill and carries on out of the other side to end arbitrarily on a secondary mound above the north-east entrance. In section it is L-shaped reinforced concrete but the other side is open, protecting pedestrians with metal hand-railing: another deliberate ambiguity. The other bridge is supported by unexpectedly tall steel 'goal-post' stanchions and runs diagonally from the middle of the podium level across into the trees.

The effect of the mounded topography to the north is of a great green blanket. Its high points are bare grass, its lower reaches planted with Mediterranean pine into which the goal-post bridge disappears on its way to the north-east entrance.

There are two square sections of the old building retained at the north and south ends of the site. At one time they had possibly been vaulted. Now open to the sky, they read as an almost Moorish pair of pavilions formed by intersecting brick arches. The

central module of both the pavilions has a shallow pool. Freixes has replaced the old brick columns with thin cast-iron replacements set on square stone pads at the four corners of the central pools, in the middle of which are specially commissioned sculptures.

The street outside the site has been planted with an avenue to the west and on the north-east is a small external entrance plaza set at a diagonal which follows the geometry of the streets on that side. To the north of this entrance a tall circular chimney has been left embedded in the wall as a reminder of the history of the area. The arched openings have been reinforced with new brickwork to above head-height and people pass between them, immediately to mount the wide stairs directly behind to the beginning of the hilly slopes. A longer narrower plaza on the same diagonal provides access to the site from the south-east at podium level. Two steel-framed pylons of glass bricks, triangular in section, light up at night, both illuminating and signposting the park.

(*Above*) A waterfall cascades from the side of the 'aqueduct' into the pool below, from which water jets emerge: a sheet of water flows down, while sprays jet up. The waterfall stops dangerously close to the opening through which emerges the overhead walkway leading left to the mound.

(*Left*) One of the two pavilions created from remnants of the old building. The original brick column supports have been replaced with cast-iron columns set on pads in the new square pool, its centrepiece an enigmatic sculpture.

3.3
Dan Kiley
FOUNTAIN PLAZA
Dallas, Texas
1985
for Crismark Property

Downtown Dallas is a collection of commercial towers, heavily geared to motor traffic and very hot in summer. Dan Kiley's Fountain Plaza was conceived as a place for people to walk and sit in the ground-level space around the base of I.M. Pei's 60-storey twisted glass Allied Bank tower. The trapezoidal perimeter of the building responds to the angled perimeter of a hotel site on the west and sits diagonally across the site, which rises 4 metres/13 ft from the south-east to the north-west. It is bounded on the north and east by the Dallas street grid. The original proposal for the site was for a pair of trapezoidal buildings, one to the north and the other to the south, separated by a central plaza and a roughly symmetrical landscape formation at ground level. At the moment the scheme retains the central plaza and the water landscaping around the I.M. Pei tower to the north.

Kiley established a double 5-metre/15-ft grid across the whole site regardless of level, the second grid shifted one half module diagonally. The intersections of the first grid were marked by 200 circular planters for bald cypresses and those of the second grid by bubbling fountains. It is essentially a traditional quincunx formation, with a fountain instead of the central tree.

Seventy per cent of the site is taken up by water. Certain areas are allocated for hard paving, such as the central plaza, its approach path from the street on the east, the flights of stairs from the north and an island reached from one end of the building. Hard surfaces are either access routes or places for sitting out and eating.

Kiley accommodated the changes in level, mostly in the north-west section of the site, by creating a set of stepping pools cascading water over their edges down to the level of the water surrounding the main central plaza. In some cases along the north the change of level is considerable, with water pouring six or eight feet from between the circular planters. In most cases the change of level between pools is 60

cm/two feet, with the top edge of the planters just above water. The impression is somewhat of a large grove of meticulously spaced trees growing out of the water. The cascading pools are made up of a number of 5-metre/15-ft grid squares connected to form irregular shapes, which create a deliberately complex flow and fall of sheets of water. The planters closest to the tower are filled with yellow bulbs in season.

The pedestrian approach to the building from the north-east, off Ross Avenue, is a 3-metre/10-ft drop down five flights of stairs to the level of the main plaza and the eastern boundary of Field Street. Each separate flight of stairs is accompanied by the appropriate changes in water-level in the adjoining pools. The experience is of a walk down between a series of noisy, heavily planted rapids and bubbling waterspouts to a placid orthogonal ensemble of paving and water and fountains which has been likened, not without some justification, to swamp-land.

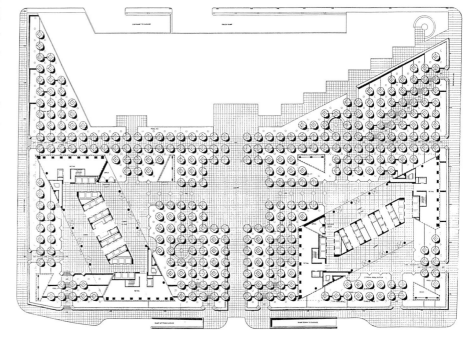

(*Below*) The imagery evoked is akin to a wild set of rapids rushing through a landscape. Yet the ensemble is based on a rigid orthogonal geometry laid over the sloping contours of the site.

(*Right*) From the street the building appears to rise out of a bed of water gridded by the bald cypresses, in their circular planters, and the bubbling fountains.

Aerial view from the west: I.M. Pei's office building (*left*) and the geometric fountain (*centre*), flanked by the formal avenues on either side. The pyramids adjacent to the office building are a later addition.

In the main plaza the paving pattern follows the primary grid but without the tree planters. Nine square modules in area, the central module has more than 200 water nozzles in its floor. They are computer-programmed to create a variety of geometric shapes in water: cubes, triangular solids, three-dimensional crosses and a series of changing shapes as well. The effect is somewhere between a water-ballet and a three-dimensional water composition. The water forms rise dramatically straight out of the paving, draining quickly away between the joints: Kiley has created a way of developing apparently solid shapes which disappear in an instant to form a succession of others.

Kiley's design is fundamentally classical, in the sense that he has created an extraordinary space and sound environment based on a rigidly imposed geometric order which pays no attention to the topography of the site. The grid defines the normal order and arrangement of elements: water, planters and fountains. Where it is appropriate they are left out – for example, trees and planters do not appear on the central plaza and approach path, nor are there trees adjacent to the tower, nor water on walkways

and sitting-out areas, where it is replaced by paving. The changes in pool levels are created by joining up the grid-lines with physical barriers. Yet the scheme is able to suggest the rush and bubble of upland waterways, the dark serenity of marshlands, the endless leafy canopies of such public landscapes as the Tuileries. In the evening the bubbling fountains and waterfalls across the whole site are illuminated from beneath. The combination of lights, modified by the movement and sound of the water, provides an unexpected interlude in this utilitarian area of town.

(*Above left*) At plaza level planters form a regular ordering pattern with the addition of water-jets located at the centre of each grid-square. They are in a sense the fifth element in a traditional Renaissance quincunx array.

(*Above*) The 90-degree geometry of Kiley's grid slides happily underneath the 60-degree geometry of Pei's building.

3.4
Bernard Tschumi
PARC DE LA VILLETTE
Paris
1983 to date
for the French Ministry of Culture

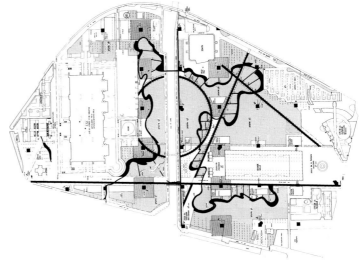

In 1983 Bernard Tschumi won the competition for the design of the Parc de la Villette. The site, in north-east Paris, had been a major cattle-market; it had a large nineteenth-century market hall near the south-east corner and the broad Ourcq canal more or less bisecting the site on an east–west axis. South of the east end of the canal was a big pop concert hall, the City of Music, and in the north section the recently built Museum of Science, a vast hi-tech structure in concrete and glass in front of which floated a giant stainless-steel sphere, the Géode (in fact an IMAX cinema). The brief was to create a significant public space, perhaps the first in Paris since Alphand's parks in the mid-nineteenth century.

Tschumi's design is a mixture of architecture and landscape. The architecture consists of 40 *folies*, bright red constructions in a deliberately Constructivist style. Some of them are functional – tea rooms, a crèche, information booths and so on – and some have associated buildings and gardens. Others are simply constructions, follies in the real sense – some with stairways leading nowhere, others simply the basic red 10-metre/30-ft cube on which all the *folies* are based, with enigmatic structural elements threaded through them.

The *folies* are arranged on a precise 120-metre/130-yard square grid laid arbitrarily over the whole site: for example, where the grid runs through the great science museum, *folies* are constructed on intersection points inside the building. Those on the gridline to the immediate south of the canal are linked by a covered path; the covering also serves as an elevated walkway, with stairs leading down to ground level at each *folie*. A second walkway, running north–south down the west side of the site past the old restored nineteenth-century *halle*, is not quite aligned with the grid. The adjacent *folies* and their associated buildings on this route serve the purpose of information booths, markets, workshops, restaurants, an open-air cinema, dance areas, video and computer rooms, greenhouses, thermal baths, a martial arts centre, a library and exhibition areas.

The second main linear element is a set of tree-lined avenues, some arranged along existing short-cuts, others in deliberately formal layouts – for example, a great broken circular avenue crosses the canal in front of the science museum. But it is offset to the west; here, formality avoids the kind of design logic which would call for the Géode to serve as the primary focus of the circle.

Through his apparently ordered network of buildings and avenues runs a serpentine path, the Path of Thematic Gardens. It links a series of recreational spaces, gardens, small bathing pools, picnic areas, allotments and educational areas, some of which are associated with individual *folies*. Many of the thematic gardens have been designed by other landscape designers – rather in the manner of an architect calling in interior designers to produce individual rooms. Tschumi has likened the thematic gardens to the frames in a movie film where the sound-track is the visitors' path and the continuity – the promenade, street furniture and planting – is provided by Tschumi. The predominant ground surface is the standard Parisian compacted earth and gravel but some areas are grassed and some have stabilized surfaces for ball games.

Tschumi has deployed some of the individual elements from the great Parisian parks: the vast scale, linear vistas, avenue formations, the serpentine routes used extensively by Alphand. Even the *folies* come from a late-nineteenth-century French and English landscape tradition. There is, too, the fact that unlike those parks the La Villette park is directed at enabling people to do more than stroll and admire trees. It is designed for a multiplicity of events, from pop concerts through playing educational games at the science museum or shopping in the restored market hall to the wide variety of small-scale activities which Tschumi had devised.

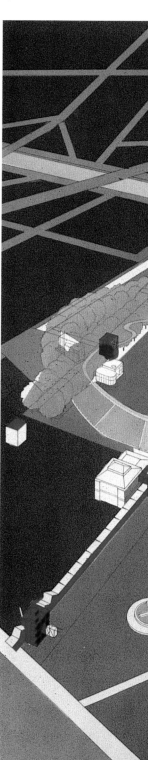

(*Opposite and below*)
Plan and aerial view of the master plan, showing how Tschumi has deliberately avoided conventional development of the site. The north–south axis has been shifted to one side, upsetting received notions of order, while lines of walkways and the siting of the *folies* are overlaid in a disjunctive, unrelated way. The *folies* are precisely positioned on a 120-metre square grid. Where the grid runs through the science museum (*middle top*) the *folies* are constructed on grid intersection points within the building.

(*Right*) The suspended walkway along the Ourcq canal defines the major east–west line with *folies* behind.

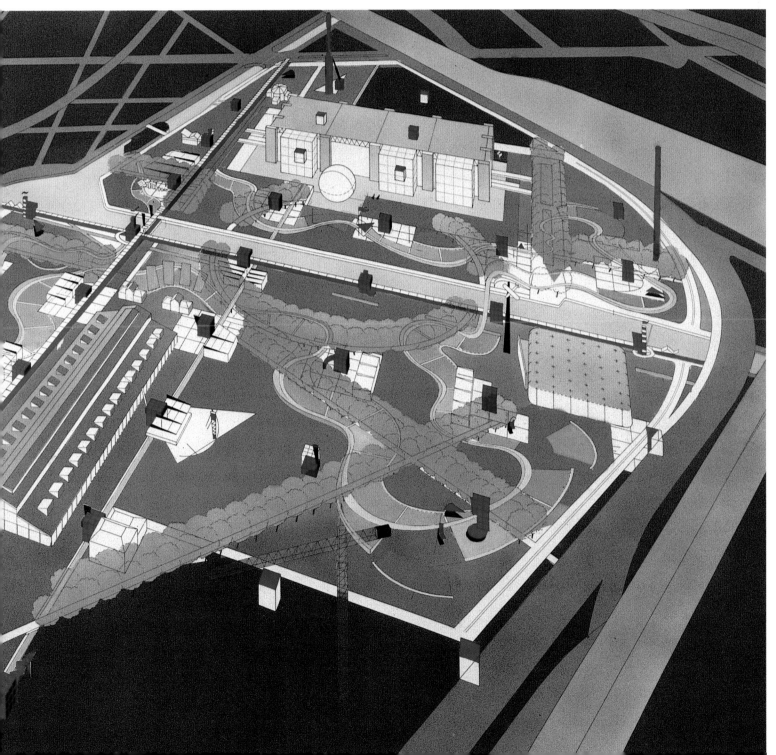

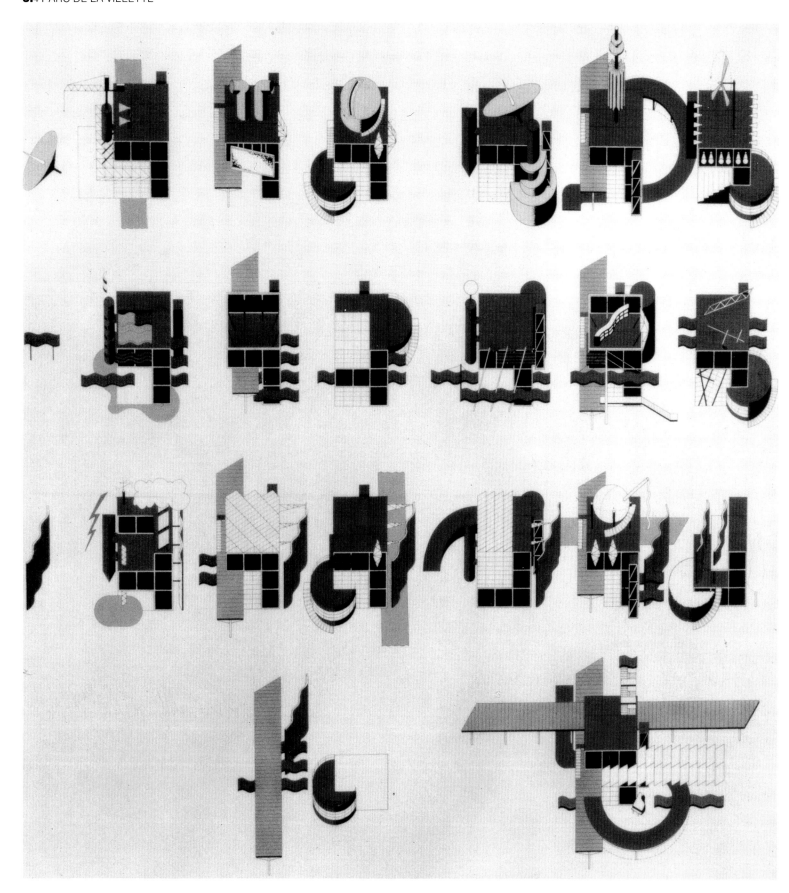

(Opposite and above)
The architectural
elements in Tschumi's
plan are 40 *folies*: **bright**
red constructions, some
of which are genuinely
functionless and
enigmatic (above**) while**
other are functional:
they may be tea-houses,
information booths or
crèches.

Yet the park's scheme is based on other purely design considerations. Tschumi's fundamental idea was to question the notion of order, to investigate the concepts of disjunction in which apparently orderly systems are laid over each other in a deliberately unrelated way. He describes it as a 'disjunctive strategy . . . in which facts never quite connect and relations of conflict are carefully maintained, rejecting synthesis or totality'. His scheme has attempted to show that it is possible to design a complex organization without resorting to traditional rules of composition, hierarchy and order. In fact the design is made up of three distinct layers. Tschumi describes these as points, lines and surfaces, each system of which is overlaid on the other without any orderly relationship between them. The 'points' are represented by the intersection of the grid-lines on which sit the *folies*. The 'lines' are the two major walkways and the system of treelined avenues with the serpentine path acting as a secondary, arbitrarily

related sub-system. The 'surfaces' are the basic ground-level materials, gravel, grass, water and planting.

The *folies* serve as a kind of reference, rather as the Métro stations do in Paris, and as servicing-points for visitors. This is not necessarily apparent on the ground, although it is clear on the drawing-board, because they are sufficiently far apart, criss-crossed by avenues of trees and curious and pleasurable in form. In any case, for the viewer seeking order there is the problem that the grid has no formal relationship with the rest of the design. The main north-south axis is skewed to one side, the serpentine path meanders in a deliberately random way through the grid and through the formal, but equally arbitrarily arranged avenues. What Tschumi has done is deliberately to abandon the design relationships which are traditionally expected in landscape – in a sense he has deconstructed the elements and reassembled them in a new and fresh way.

3.5
Alexandre Chemetoff
THE BAMBOO GARDEN
Parc de la Villette, Paris
1987
for Etablissement Public du Parc de la Villette

Alexandre Chemetoff of the Bureau des Paysages was one of the nine winners of the competition for the Parc de la Villette, which was eventually designed by Bernard Tschumi (see 3.4). Part of Tschumi's grand strategy for the park was a series of thematic gardens along a serpentine *promenade ciné-matique*. Four of these were to be located at the crossing of two major avenues. Asked to design them, Chemetoff suggested that they should be incorporated into one landscape with the theme of bamboo, the differences coming about by varying the species and incorporating the work of two artists. On an earlier commission he had come across the bamboo plantation at Anduze, in the south of France, which had been established by a collector in

the mid-nineteenth century. Bamboo needs special conditions for growing successfully, so Chemetoff decided to create a sunken landscape sheltered from the prevailing winds and with a radiating south-facing wall, creating its own micro-climate.

His design has a 6-metre/20-ft-deep retaining wall running across the north boundary beside the main avenue, which is lined with plane trees. The sinuous west and south boundary follows Tschumi's *prome-nade*, banking steeply down towards the retaining wall. Three parallel catwalks cross the 2,800-square-metres/30,000-square-ft valley at a skew, joining the east–west avenue with the thematic path to the south. In the east corner is a sound garden by Bernard Leitner, two concentric concrete cylinders with eight grilles and horizontal slits at high level through which trickles water in curtains down to an internal perimeter water-trough. Taped music wraps the visitor in gentle sound. The cylinders are the same height as the ground level outside, which contributes

(*Opposite*) One of the three walkways crossing the Bamboo Garden, following the alignment of the old sewage pipe slung underneath.

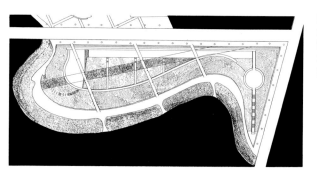

(*Left*) Plan: the north retaining wall across the top supports one of the main promenades of the park outside.

(*Left*) Contrasted bands of pebbles on the path along the north retaining wall follow a diagonal ordering system. The retaining wall has a built-in system of drainage which copes with the high local water-table.

to the notion of a landscape scooped out of the flat earth, retaining traces of an underground world of times gone by. The cylinders are broken on the north–south axis, and a great flight of stairs with water cascading in channels on either side leads down through a long bamboo grove from the park to the south. At the opposite, western end of the site a long semicircular flight of steps leads from the outside ground level through lush bamboo planting down to the base of the valley.

The 120-metre/400-ft-long wall is made from interlocking concrete panels fitted between the upper exposed sections of circular retaining piles. A walkway parallel with the main avenue is cantilevered over the top, forming a kind of blind arcade. Three levels of horizontal troughs span the space between each column. Wisteria is trained over the concrete, but pruned back to keep the underlying structure visible. Apart from maintaining the integrity of the adjoining avenue and its row of planes, the south-facing wall serves as a heat trap, slightly warming the whole sunken area. Additional light is cast into darker areas of the planting below by a set of large-diameter night-time lighting reflectors mounted on the wall. The existence of a fairly high water-table, probably due to leakage from the nearby Canal Ourcq, was not initially encouraging for the idea of a sunken garden. But Chemetoff incorporated a large number of circular land-drains at regular intervals into the wall. Seepage water falls randomly from these pipes into the horizontal troughs and thence to a channel at the base of the retaining wall. It is connected to a narrow canal

winding across the middle of the site. The whole landscape is watered by high-level jets which spray at programmed intervals.

A long consolidated gravel path runs at the foot of the wall. Towards the east the plain gravel becomes diagonal bands of black and grey pebbles, a design by the artist Daniel Buren; a narrow curving concrete channel at a lower level breaks into the edge of the path. It forms a sinuous thread through the middle of the landscape. Three parallel ramping dry channels from the south edge of the path are connected to it at intervals. With the exception of the wisteria on the retaining wall the planting is entirely bamboo, with 40 different species. A band of black bamboo crosses the site diagonally from east to west, aligning with Buren's diagonal banding in the long path below the retaining wall.

Excavation revealed that the site was crossed by three main sewers. Instead of attempting to divert them Chemetoff deployed them as a species of urban archaeology, using them as the alignment for his catwalks, the supporting columns of which carry the drains several feet below. Buren wrapped sections of the pipe with black tape where the diagonal band of black bamboo passed underneath.

Chemetoff has created a secret garden in the flat plain of the park which in many ways reflects the ordering system of the whole scheme, with its layering of independent geometries and patterning, bamboo species planting, gravel, channels, paths, catwalks, real and implied urban archaeology – all of which collide or relate arbitrarily with each other to form a congruous whole.

(*Left*) The sound garden by Bernard Leitner is the focus of a long descending flight of stairs from the ground level of La Villette above.

(*Right*) In the depths of the all-bamboo landscape the winding channel leads off into the foreground, with the straight path below the north retaining wall visible under the high-level catwalk.

4 RELATING TO ARCHITECTURE

Landscape and architecture, architecture and land-scape: the two have historically belonged to each other, whether it be the little architectural set-pieces in the eighteenth-century garden at Stowe, England, or the hard architectural setting of Arata Isozaki's contemporary Tsukuba Centre in Japan. With some justification, landscape designers complain that many contemporary commissions are merely tacked on at the end of the construction of a building as a kind of decorative accent – or, more likely, to mitigate the visual effects of a less than talented piece of architectural design. Landscape construction cannot normally start until building work is completed, and there is some truth in the companion complaint that landscape budgets are regularly slashed when the building turns out to be over budget. Very occasionally landscape designers form part of the initial design team, as at the NMB Bank in Amsterdam, and in some cases start off as the master-planners of a site. In other cases, such as Carlo Scarpa's Brion cemetery, the architect and landscape designer are the same person, the design being conceived as an integrated whole; Isozaki's Tsukuba Centre is also an integrated conception. At Stockley Park and the awkwardly named Capability Green, one designer takes the view that the best surroundings for a business park are essentially sylvan, while the other, Robert Holden, feels that orthogonal architecture calls for a formal setting. Arthur Erickson has achieved an integration by carpeting the architecture with landscape.

Robson Square, Vancouver, Canada.

123

4.1
Arup Associates and Bernard Ede Associates

STOCKLEY PARK
London
1988
for Stockley plc

Master-planned by Arup Associates with the landscape designers Bernard Ede Associates, Stockley Park was originally a big rubbish dump north of London's Heathrow Airport. It is now a 36-hectare/ 90-acre business park, with 100 hectares/250 acres of golf-course, playing-fields and parkland. The arrangement of the site with the business park on the south is partly to do with the need for close access to the nearby motorway, partly to provide a green buffer zone from the surrounding suburb and partly because the original topography of the southern part of the site suggested the creative deployment of water.

Under the landfill it had several shallow valleys leading to the old Grand Union canal running along the southern border. It was necessary to construct attenuation ponds for storm-water run-off from the adjacent area, and the designers turned these into a set of linear lakes around which the new buildings are set.

Creating the development called for transferring landfill, dumped to an average depth of 9 metres/30 ft during the last 50 years, from the south part of the site to the north where it forms the basic structure for an undulating naturalistic landscape. Problems associated with the methane generated by the rubbish were solved by alternating layers of landfill with site clay, with a topsoil of sludge cake and clay which forms a semi-permeable membrane. In this northern area the planting is primarily forest material: alders, poplar, willow, oak and ash. In the southern section a major constraint was a noisy stone-crushing plant and a helicopter maintenance workshop immediately to the south of the canal; major mounding and screen planting had therefore to be installed immediately north of the canal.

The buildings are arranged in four north–south groupings separated by small lakes and on the west by a through road. Each of the buildings has a large car-parking area at its back, with high, clipped hornbeam hedges creating outdoor rooms conceal-

(***Below left***) **Plan of the park, with the top area dedicated to public landscape and the building development across the bottom above the old canal and around the lakes.**

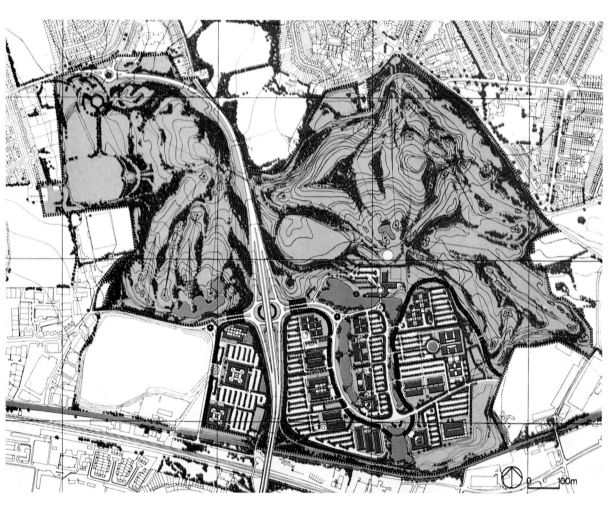

The heavily planted entrance to one of the buildings.

A lakeside view with the central facility building (*left*).

ing not only the cars but much of the rear of the buildings. Within these enclosing walls whitebeams provide a canopy for the cars. Hornbeam has also been used to enclose private gardens in the spaces between and around the buildings, which are planted with lower evergreen trees and shrubs such as cotoneaster and juniper arranged informally. None of the buildings is particularly assertive and none more than three storeys high, so their presence is further diminished by the enclosing planting. The hornbeam around the rear of the car parks is clipped internally but on the outside is left to form a long unpruned mass of thick hedging.

The regular geometry of each building and its car park is mitigated by staggering building-lines but more importantly by establishing a winding circulation pattern for cars and pedestrians through the site, around the perimeter of the lakes. The pedestrian route has a canopy of paired clipped limes broken only at the entrance to each building, where there are hornbeam screens edging access roads.

The business park is planted formally with semi-mature species directly into clay or topsoil. Planes are used at the entrance and at strategic positions where they can form a visual stop. There are maples along secondary routes, and limes around the curving pedestrian route.

The design has been likened to a classic English garden. It is enclosed except on the north, where it runs up into 'natural' woodland planting. The formal hedges, somewhat influenced by edge planting in classic French gardens, form a background to the irregular footways along the edges of the lakes. Low, unpretentious bridges cross necks of water, some sections of which are formed as low falls leading to the southernmost lake. It is an attempt at creating a sylvan, traditional setting for pedestrians walking through the site with contrasting formal entrances leading to the buildings, not entirely un-reminiscent of an English village scene.

(*Above, far left, left and right*) A somewhat villagey landscape environment for the orthogonal forms of the buildings.

4.2
J'ørn Copijn and Peter Rawstorne
NMB BANK

Amsterdam
1987
for NMB Bank

The Dutch landscape architect Jø'rn Copijn and the British designer Peter Rawstorne were asked to join the design team for the new headquarters building of NMB, the third biggest bank in the Netherlands, located in a new commercial and housing development in the south-east outskirts of Amsterdam. It is very unusual for such designers to be involved at this early stage, but the architect Ton Alberts and the bank had decided that integrating the specialist team from the beginning was the most satisfactory way of working. A number of the design team, including Copijn, Rawstorne and Alberts, and some of the bank's board members were anthroposophists, and the ten clusters of low-rise sloping and curving brick-clad surfaces making up the building complex reflect the Rudolf Steineresque faith to which they subscribe.

Because each member of the design team was charged with responsibility to comment and contribute ideas outside their particular specialisms, the final design has a built-in organic quality in which surfaces, forms, decoration and landscape are remarkably integrated. It also meant that trees and plants and rocks could be located at will because their positions were known in advance and the engineers could design the supporting structure to carry them. Similarly, the architects knew where internal trees and plants were to be located and planned for them to grow out of the floor rather than having to put them in planters. The landscape design is also ecologically innovative in the sense that insects have been introduced to control pests and aviaries set up to house a variety of birds which feed on pests and help pollinate plants. The building is also energy-efficient: it has been reckoned to have the lowest energy consumption in the world, to no small extent because of its form and orientation.

The landscape design permeates the building – Copijn's planting around the site, several set-piece enclosed landscapes, a rooftop garden, the irrigation system for the lavish indoor planting, as well as water features and lighting produced commercially by Rawstorne in the UK. The most dramatic indoor feature is a snaking 45-metre/150-ft-long bronze-coated handrail to several ramps from the third level of the building down to one of the entrances. Its other function is to serve as the path for a narrow cascading stream which feeds a water-garden and at the lower level ends in a large pool.

The water-garden, enclosed by building on the south, starts from a small circular pool, half inside and half outside the building, from which it runs across an adjacent single-storey roof and doubles

(Opposite) **The Japanese garden, designed by J'ørn Copijn, is half enclosed around the left by several clusters. On two levels, one the roof of an integral car park, the transition is achieved with black, water-stained rocks over which the stream from an upper pool cascades into a pebbled shallow pool at the lower level.**

(Below) **Plan: the 'clusters' of sculptural brickwork are linked by an internal landscape path and at the same time enclose outdoor landscapes.**

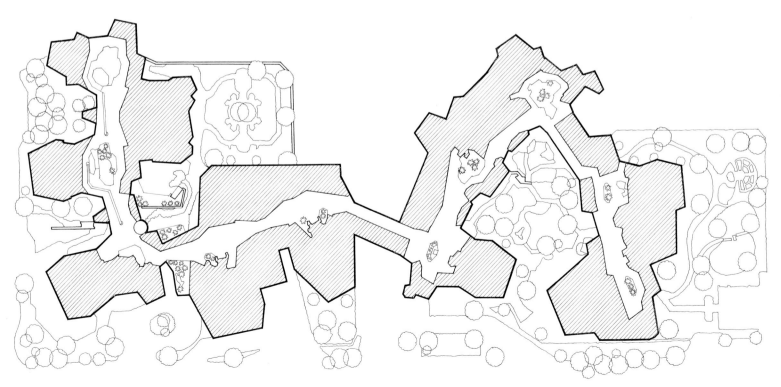

back down an elaborate brick cascade to a large shallow pool at the next level down. A greenhouse in one corner serves as a display area for the pot plants which have to be brought inside during winter. Immediately to the south but visually separated from it is a small landscaped area adjacent to the directors' entrance, composed of large flat granite slabs, split as they came from the quarry, and fine-leaved plants. Its centrepiece is a large sculpture in acid-etched and rubbed red stone concrete from whose edges water swirls down to the stone and earth below.

The east section of the complex almost entirely encloses a more serene landscape, which has been dubbed the 'Japanese' garden by the bank. Facing south, it is on two levels, the upper section being the roof of a car park with a still pool and Japanese trees. Water from the upper pool falls over the edge, formed from massive, black-stained stone slabs, to a lower shallow pool criss-crossed by stone paths edged with large water-washed pebbles and carefully placed pieces of stone. It is a design which pays loose respect to the Japanese tradition of deploying a simple palette of found natural objects, water and delicately located accents of coloured planting and foliage.

On the other side of the northernmost building-cluster is the swamp garden on top of a car park: heather, willows and wild plants such as arnica are arranged on a foundation of peat around several wetlands-style pools. Elsewhere around the perimeter of the complex there is heavy ground planting along the south and a casual arrangement of plane trees in the shopping plaza in front of the main entrance to the north.

Much is said by landscape designers and architects about creating a synthesis of their skills. But in practice landscape design tends to occur after the critical decisions are made about the building's form, and landscape construction has to wait until the greater part of building construction has been completed. At NMB there has been from the beginning a commonality of visual preferences and of design intentions which has produced an unusually well-integrated fusion of building, landscape, environmental controls, and art – for which the bank set aside more than one per cent of the total construction costs. That is not to say that there is a direct consonance between the form of the building and the landscape. There has, however, been a deliberate attempt to maintain a degree of continuity in terms of colour, and sometimes the use of similar materials such as brick and bronze-coated reconstituted stone, which reflects some of the eaves detailing on a number of the low veranda roofs around the complex.

The NMB complex does not offer typical conditions for landscaping. The building and some of the water details are idiosyncratic, and would not be repeatable in the vast majority of commercial circumstances; but they square neatly with the philosophy of the client.

(*Opposite*) The water garden, enclosed by clusters to the north-west of the complex. Peter Rawstorne's biomorphic concrete shapes provide sculptured stages for this complicated cascade.

(*Above left*) Stepping-stones across the pool in the Japanese garden and the surrounding planting are reminiscent of the original models.

(*Above*) A formal space by one of the directors' entrances, geometry contrasting with naturalistic forms.

4.3
Arthur Erickson Architects
ROBSON SQUARE
Vancouver, Canada
1983

for British Columbia Buildings Corporation

Robson Square encompasses three city blocks in central Vancouver. It is a three-dimensional urban park incorporated into a small megastructure which contains the city's law courts and government offices together with a cinema, theatre, exhibition area, food fair, plaza, an outdoor skating rink, several upper-level public parks, a wooded hill, waterfalls, a long formal rooftop pool and thousands of feet of linear planter-boxes and garden beds. The Vancouver art gallery occupies most of the northern block, its classical portico serving as the distant focus of the whole scheme's main axis. Robson Square is an enormous ensemble of concrete terraces, stairs in ziggurat formation, water, large and small spaces and masses of foliage and tree planting. It represents an integration of architecture and landscape in which the one penetrates, surrounds and complements the other, an ensemble which was designed to lift the quality of urban life in a relatively drab commercial setting.

At the south the complex starts with the great sloping glass roof of the law courts. Seven levels high, the courts and offices are arranged under the glass canopy in a series of plant-festooned terraces which rise following the profile of the roof. At the lowest level is a wide public concourse. It leads north across a bridge over the first cross road and into a

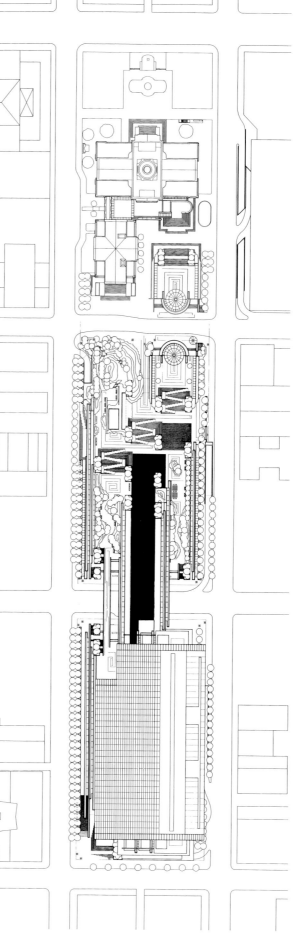

(*Left*) Plan: at the bottom is the glass roof of the law courts with the roof-top pool carried over the cross road. The bridge to the left is for pedestrians. The zigzags to the north of the pool are Erickson's 'stramps', running down to the low-level civic square which leads under the next cross road to the forecourt of the art gallery.

(*Far left*) Robson Square from the north: the law courts at the rear, the pool over staggered government offices and Vancouver city art gallery in the foreground.

132

(*Right*) Heavy foliage is
draped over the linear
concrete planters at the
south entrance to the
law-court section of the
complex. It continues
inside under the great
glass roof.

(*Above*) From the city art gallery, one wing of which is visible (*right*), the sunken civic square is a bustling place in its own right and marks the beginning of the journey across three city blocks to the distant law courts through a carpet of landscape.

(*Left*) Visible only from high level, the long, formal roof-top pool comes as an unexpected vision for people walking around the complex.

(*Above right*) The triangular profile of the megastructure lessens its bulk and the strips of planters contribute to a feeling of horizontality.

park at high level alongside a 90-metre/300-ft pool one level higher, roofing the three-storey government offices. It leads to a series of stairs and ramps beside three cascades down to the sunken civic square, which extends under the second cross road to the forecourt of the Vancouver art gallery, an early twentieth-century neo-classical building which was originally the city law courts. The wide tunnel to this third block is marked by big open plexiglass domes on either side of the road which provide some protection for the wintertime ice-skating rink.

The large law-court structure at the south end has a deliberately distinctive form commensurate with its importance. Its characteristically truncated triangle cross-section is repeated in more modest form in the office block, as are its long horizontal planter-boxes marking the edge of each terrace.

The vast, sloping, space-frame roof of tinted glass covers a long public concourse with three internal terraces rising up under its higher side. They serve as waiting areas for the courts on these levels. The long horizontal edges and intermediate planters are hung with trailing plants; trees in large pots are arranged along the lower side. The internal environment is regulated by a combination of solar heat collection and control systems and underground water heat-sinks. Rooftop tanks for the waterfall system double up as the supply for the sprinkler system.

The 90-metre/300-ft-long pool flows over a partly glassed deck, with the transparent roof of the top floor of the office facilities below. The pool is bordered by formal garden beds with associated linear planting troughs at the lower edge of the scarcely visible canted windows to the top office floor. The same detail of canted glazing and linear troughs crammed with trailing plants occurs on lower floors. The three waterfall pools have underwater roof-lights and there are windows behind the

cascades: rather charmingly, the room behind one of these dramatic water-washed windows is the city wedding registry.

Several of the terraces on rooftops on either side of the pool are actually small parks planted out with substantial trees and ground-cover. At the end of the long pool the water cascades in a great sheet down into a big reflecting pool, down another level to an L-shaped pool and thence sideways to yet another pool, with a cascade down to a street-level pool beside the main east pedestrian access to the sunken plaza. Alongside the cascades are three sets of what became known in the Erickson office as stramps. They are wide stairways with ramps zigzagging across them. They emphasize the diagonal design theme, but their main function is to allow disabled people to use the upper and lower levels of the landscape. North-west of the stramp flights parts of the public facilities have been bermed, creating a small heavily wooded hill.

The perimeter of the landscape is bordered by long stretches of planting stepping up the sides of the architectural elements: a row of trees on either side of the pavement behind which are terraces of laurels at street level, changing to terraces of pine and bamboo groves, maple and dogwood with juniper along the long pool. The change represents the changes found in planting at increasingly high altitudes. Hanging planters in the big concourse of the law courts have, unexpectedly, roses spilling from them. The wooded hill at the approach to the art gallery has rhododendrons, pines and maples.

(*Opposite*) The waterfalls at the end of the long pool with their adjacent 'stramps' leading down to the civic square.

(*Above*) One of the intermediate gardens on the central block. The long pool is on the roof-top to the right.

(*Top left*) **Dense foliage draped down the sides of the horizontal planters overshadows the windows of the government offices inside.**

(*Left below*) **One of the intimate spaces at Robson Square, unexpected and almost sylvan.**

(*Above*) **Erickson's 'stramps', a combination of ramp and stairway, lead up from the civic square, eventually reaching the level of the pool.**

Unlike other landscapes which have been added to cover up dull sections of construction, Robson Square was conceived as a multi-level landscape and a work of architecture at the same time. There are certain ostensible perversities in, for example, placing a dramatically large pool at a high level, visible only from a few public spaces at the end of the law courts, and in creating a small hill when the level below is plainly an open area with visible structural columns. But artifice, unexpectedness and surprise are part of the great Western tradition of landscape. What Erickson has done, with his landscape adviser, Cornelia Oberlandser, is to drape a landscape cloak over a structure which has been cunningly devised to accept it, and to work as a piece of functioning building design.

(*Opposite*) **The main pool ends with a pair of waterfalls behind which are public rooms, including the registry office. The roof-lights are outlined beneath the water of the second pool.**

4.4
M. Paul Friedberg
WINTER GARDEN
Niagara Falls, New York State, USA
1977
for Niagara Falls Redevelopment Agency

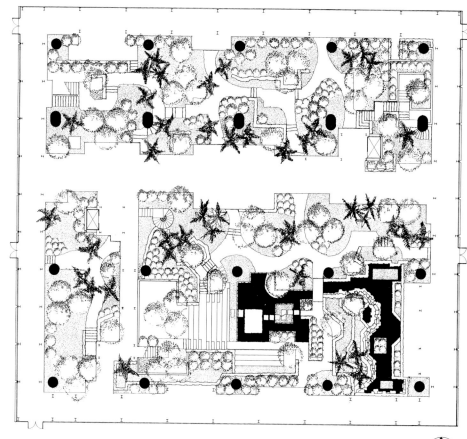

Run down, and facing severe competition from the Canadian city across the border, Niagara Falls obtained Federal urban renewal funds for its regeneration. The city needed a major facility which would act as the centrepiece for subsequent development, which would draw tourists to the US side during the long, bleak winter months and would form a year-round attraction for residents. As part of this, a great winter-garden structure by the architect Cesar Pelli was constructed, straddling a new downtown mall along Main Street, the spine of new hotel and other development leading to the Falls. The landscape architect M. Paul Friedberg's brief was to create a semi-tropical landscape environment which incorporated facilities for performances and exhibitions.

The structure is a dramatic greenhouse 53 metres/175 ft long, 47 metres/155 ft wide and 33 metres/107 ft high at the top of its zigzagging glass roof. The mall leading to the Falls through the winter-garden building has a formal east section relating to the more formal buildings around it. It is flanked on each side by an outer row of red maples and an inner row of Bradford pear trees, both of which produce colourful blossom in spring and foliage colour in autumn. It is paved in a mixture of asphalt block and banded brick, with the trees set in traditional round tree-grates and street furniture in traditional timber-slatted metal. The western section of the mall is less formal. It is broken up with rectangles of lawn, informal tree planting and a children's playground, and it has spectacular views of the Falls to the west. A single row of red maples on each side maintains continuity with the line of the east mall.

Inside the great glazed space of the winter-garden there is a complete change of environment. Brick-paved paths take visitors through the lush sub-tropical vegetation to the western mall beyond. Alongside and overhead are a series of metal catwalks encircling and crossing this landscape, providing views of the planting and topography below. There are more than 175 different varieties of sub-tropical

(*Top and above*) An east–west section through the lower part of the plan, showing how the two major areas of water have been created by mounding the surroundings. Symbols on the plan (*above*) indicate the position of the perimeter upper-level walkways and catwalks.

(*Opposite, top*) From the Falls the Pelli glasshouse reads clearly as an enclosure of a section of the main thoroughfare.

(*Right*) The main axis passes through the greenhouse, with sitting areas beside the landscape set-pieces.

(*Below*) Part of the external landscape: a children's play area adjacent to the west section of the mall.

plants, including 60-foot-high palms, corn plants, figs, papyrus, Chinese evergreens and dwarf dragon trees. They are to be found in hanging baskets as heavy ground cover, or as screening planting and in set-piece spaces. This internal landscape has a modestly botanical function and many of the 7,500 plants are labelled.

The main path cuts across the building, dividing the landscape into two sections, the south area twice that of the north. The path has small nooks for people to sit and watch and is crossed by one of the upper-level walkways. Behind the walls of lush vegetation is a series of meandering paths and spaces, small hills and dales with sometimes dramatically changing levels, small stepped terraces, pools, quiet sitting areas and specialist gardens.

One such is the arid garden in the north-west corner of the scheme. Mulched with gravel, it has the quality of a desert environment, stocked with 40 different varieties of cacti and succulents: *Cereus peruvianus*, zamia, cardboard palm, Piller cactus and various species of opuntias, sedums and echeverias. In

(*Left*) The western end of the glasshouse and its luxuriant plants in winter.

(*Below*) The eastern section of the mall leading through the glasshouse is lined with red maples and has an inner avenue of pear-trees.

(*Opposite*) The 'grotto' limestone rocks serve as a dividing spine between the performance pool and the longer pool for aquatic plants.

the diagonally opposite corner is a grotto, more accurately a 4-metre/14-ft-high Dolomitic limestone boulder rock-face with an extensive pool at its base, the habitat for around 15 different species of aquatic plants. The ground-level pool is fed by a waterfall from a reflecting pool at the top of the rock face. The paved area by the pool under the high-level perimeter walkway can be used for sitting out at tables from the adjoining commercial facility.

On the other side of the rock face the ground is terraced down to a path which bridges a return section of the grotto pool; it leads to another major area of water surrounded by foliage, including a tall Everglades palm, one of the few palms native to the USA. The pool has a small rectangular stone island approached by stepping-stones. This is the stage for small groups, ensembles, lecturers and solo performers whose audience, up to 100, can watch from stepped stone terraces on the west and south. This semi-rural amphitheatre is the major feature of the south section, its steep west terrace rising up to the roof of a concealed rest-room to connect with one of the high-level walkways. For larger shows the pool is drained and its smooth aggregate base becomes the stage.

The primary paths in the scheme are brick, with secondary routes of irregular limestone slabs with a sand-blasted surface. Outdoor furniture is consistent with that in the outdoor malls: timber-slatted cast-iron seating, concrete bollards and low-level lighting. Winter temperatures are set at between 60 and 65 degrees F, sufficiently high for exotic plants. In summer doors are left open at both levels.

Few winter gardens have been designed since the early twentieth century, when they went out of fashion. None has been designed since then at this scale, and few ever at this level of topographical and horticultural complexity. It has meant that in the long, bitter, snowy winters Niagara Falls has a semi-tropical landscape at its heart.

(*Below*) **Aquatic plants in the eastern pool at the base of the 'grotto'.**

(*Right*) In the middle of the southern landscape block, the steps leading down to the main pool double as seating terraces for public performances on the small island stage to the far left (behind the trees).

4.5

Robert Holden

CAPABILITY GREEN

Bedfordshire, UK
1987

for Lygtun Ltd

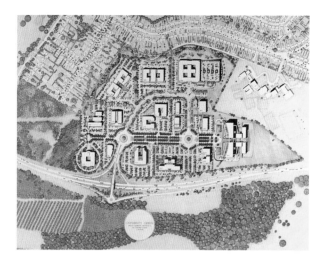

Capability Green is a 28-hectare/68-acre business-park site recently cut off by a major access road to the nearby Luton airport from the parkland of Luton Hoo, the estate designed by Capability Brown. With the new dual-carriageway road along the south and housing development to the north and west, the site was featureless, apart from a field of hedgerow oak and ash trees in the north-west and a wood to the west of broad-leaved oak, ash, birch, coppiced hornbeam and hazel, with a carpet of bluebells in springtime. An unusual legal constraint for the designers was the proximity of the airport: it was critical that bird life should be discouraged by using exotic and non-native plant material. The first major task was to create a mounded screen along the north and west sides of the park to protect locals from construction noise and the subsequent activities of the business park. The mounds are planted with fast-growing white willows, which will be removed when the slower-growing trees reach maturity. These include lime, rowan, oak, sweet chestnut and American red oak. Evergreens for winter are holm oak, box, yew and laurel. Lawns and slopes are planted with wild daffodils which flower in April.

Within the densely planted perimeter (15,000 trees were established in just the first year, and four times that number of shrubs) the basic sites and the first of the buildings were established in a series of formal layouts. About 30 per cent of the site is allocated to landscape, high for British developments. The designers took the view that using the familiar English garden approach was irrelevant to the nature of business parks. Taking the *cours* of France and the *corso* of Spain as a model, they created a formal east–west promenade the same width as the 12-metre/40-ft-wide Cours Rambourslang in Vienne and lined it with cloned Norway maples of regular shape and bright green summer foliage, set in French traditional style at a close 7.5-metre/25-ft spacing. When fully mature they will arch over, creating aisle-like avenues. Down the middle of the mall runs

a red-brick paved pedestrian route. It is a traditional European boulevard with the middle section for people rather than cars. Along the mall are 18-metre/60-ft-diameter pools with fountains marking cross axes and surrounded by roundabouts for cars.

The sides of the mall are mounded to reduce the impact of both the buildings and their surrounding car parks, and are planted with Portugal laurel and bright green *Aucuba japonica*, with golden cut-leaf elder and June-flowering *Viburnum plicatum* forming highlights. The underplanting consists of flowering herbaceous perennials including hellebore, anemone and periwinkle with bears' breeches and iris, the predominant colours of which are pale blues, whites and lilacs. Geraniums and fuchsias are bedded out in containers by steps on the mall.

Each of the individual landscapes has been designed for the buildings they surround, with one car space for every 20 square metres/213 square ft of office space. One of the early buildings is surrounded by a circular road, with concentric rings of hornbeams and Tai Haiku cherries; the subsidiary car-parking is concealed by yew hedges and compartment beds of low box enclosing green and silver hummocks of Emerald Gaiety. Elsewhere, waves of ground-cover plants with differing flowering times provide the setting for maples and shrub chestnuts. Tai Haiku cherries, used in other car parks, form the symbolic basis for a building designed for a Japanese company. It is a variety which had died out in Japan and had been rediscovered in England.

Throughout the development beech and yew are used as screens for car parks, mingled with a profuse variety of exotics, yucca, Virginia creeper, Irish yew, acacia, whitebeam, Japanese *Zelkova serrata*, laburnum, red ash, flowering crab-apple and scarlet willow. It is a landscape of dense and formal structural planting with, unusually for British landscape architecture, formal beds and gardens, masses of herbaceous plants and a concern for colour and show and complexity.

(*Top left*) The master plan of Capability Green: the main entrance off the boundary road at the bottom and the main east–west avenue parallel with it above. A curving secondary boulevard leads from the main roundabout to other buildings.

Holden declines to pretend that landscape can be maintenance-free, so there is a substantial long-term garden staff who can call on the massive resources of the old Luton Hoo estate and garden staff across the road. This establishment supplies plant stock and carries out the initial planting as each development is created.

(*Above*) **The formal pedestrian route takes the place of the central roadway in a traditional boulevard; here it is a consequential, almost processional way, with the office buildings obscured by the heavy verge planting either side of the roads.**

(*Left*) **The central boulevard from the west, with the sculpture of boxing hares.**

4.6
Arata Isozaki

TSUKUBA CIVIC CENTRE

Japan
1983

for the Development Department of Tsukuba Science City

Arata Isozaki was commissioned to design the new civic centre of Tsukuba, Japan's equivalent of Silicon Valley. His brief was to provide an hotel, office accommodation, a concert hall, an information centre and a shopping mall – the main cultural, commercial and visual elements of a city centre. Isozaki's design ranges the buildings around the south and east edge of a great plaza, which is actually the roof of the underground shopping mall. The surface is a tartan grid of ceramic tiling, created by a series of grids of different scales and colours laid over each other. It reads almost as a random series of square linear patterns on interleaved sheets of glass. Round the north and east, leading off to the east and the site of a more naturalistic park, is a double avenue of trees which are organized on the intersections of another notional grid in the paving.

In the middle of the plaza is a big ellipse carved out of the tartan; its dished base is at the shopping mall

level, with a hole in its centre. Impacted on the north-east corner of the ellipse is a group of other shapes, one the curve of a set of amphitheatre steps leading to a 'stage' at the equivalent of mezzanine level, with a straight scena down which a wall of water, generated by a vertical grid of button jets, falls in a sheet to a trough. In front of this wall, on either side, are metal pergola frames supported on massive columns of grey slate. Between this geometric shape and the ellipse is a jumble of rockwork flanked by another set of stairs. Water cascades from a basin at the top of this rock ensemble down to its base, where it is joined by another stream flowing down the stairway leading from the stage. It runs in a narrow channel to the hole in the middle of the ellipse. To the north is yet another pair of wide stairs leading down to a rectangular space at the mezzanine level; they are reminiscent of bleachers on either side of a tennis court.

The whole of this design and its surrounding buildings is a very self-conscious essay in Post-Modernism, in which Isozaki has deliberately based his design on a number of famous architects' work. In the case of the main ellipse the source is Michelangelo's Campidoglio in Rome – a direct copy but with a number of knowing differences: Isozaki's is dished and below the main plaza level where Michelangelo's is convex and raised above the surrounding area. Isozaki has reversed the colour of the paving pattern: it is dark where Michelangelo's is light, light where the original is dark. It is less like a Renaissance plaza than a Japanese garden or pool in the sense that it is, from the upper level at least, designed to be looked into rather than walked across. Perhaps most

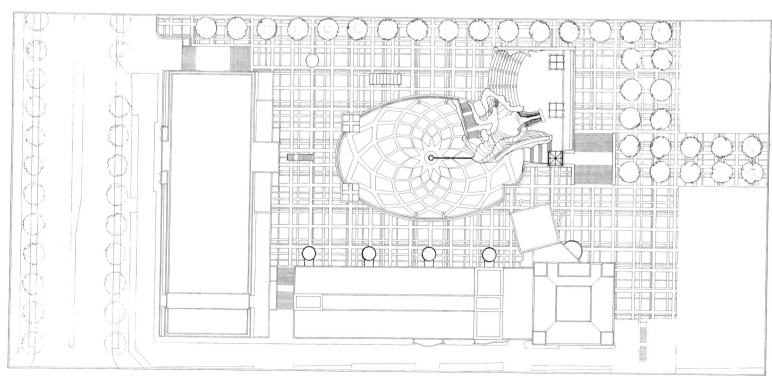

(*Opposite*) The master plan, with buildings by Isozaki on the west and south of the main plaza.

(*Above*) An aerial view from the south-east, showing the disposition of the main elements: the great ellipse with its central hole (*left*), the cascade and amphitheatre above leading to the mezzanine 'stage' with its backing water-wall.

(*Right*) A general aerial view of the centre, showing the relationship between buildings and plaza.

importantly, Michelangelo has an equestrian statue as the centrepiece: Isozaki has a drainage hole. He has gone on record as saying that, unlike the Renaissance architect working for a pope, he was working for a state which had a less clear image. 'I feel ambivalently that I would rather it didn't emerge too clearly . . . I portrayed a metaphor in which all the spatial arrangements are reversed or inverted. Everything is situated around void, descending and then vanishing into oblivion at the centre.'

The granite rockwork ensemble which breaks into the end of the ellipse and its flanking flights of stairs is topped by a giant formal basin around which rocks have been piled and bamboos planted half in and half out of the basin; an exclamation mark has been added in the form of a bronze sculpture of a laurel tree around which is draped a golden fabric scarf, a reference to the myth of Apollo and Daphne and perhaps to the central theme of reversals.

(*Left*) The transition from plaza level (*top left*), via somewhat Greek amphitheatre terracing down to the mezzanine stage, contrasts with the artificial naturalism of the piled rocks guiding the cascade from the formal basin.

(*Above*) The bronze laurel tree with its golden fabric scarf stands enigmatically at the top of the cascade stairway.

The south flight has intimations of Baroque formality, with two intermediate landings. The north staircase is wide and formal, leading from a framework dome at stage level. It serves as a pivotal point: north to the stepped bleachers, east into the shopping complex below podium level and south to the floor of the ellipse. Its formality is broken on one side by a rough rock edging, on the other side of which is a group of stepped, contoured layers of a local stone serving as a wide, irregular watercourse. It is fed by two water sources: one the rocky cascade from the basin, the other a slow stream cut into the eastern end of the stage. Sheeting thinly over an intermediate plateau, the water runs down to an irregular pool and thence via the slot-like channel to the maw of the central drain.

Isozaki has created in a sense an anti-landscape in which the unifying theme is the ambivalently juxtaposed regular grid of the main pavement and the formal geometry of the central ellipse. One end has had a bite taken out of it, part of the hollow formalized and the rest filled in with a jumble of rocks, stairways and water.

Taken together with the high Post-Modern eclecticism of the surrounding buildings Isozaki's hard landscape at Tsukuba represents one deliberate, extreme direction in environmental thinking whose meaning and intentions may not be immediately apparent (or, given the symbolism of the central hole, acceptable) to the lay visitor. Yet the very high quality of materials and their execution – and the sheer pleasure of much of the visual imagery – mean that the landscape works on its own terms.

(*Above*) View into the sunken plaza and its central hole, blandly swallowing up the water which a few metres upstream is full of incident and surprise.

(*Right*) Rockwork with a variety of visual and symbolic values: in the foreground it is carefully cut and layered, one section serving as stairway, the other as watercourse with the water spread thinly over the surface. Beyond, the same material is cut and laid in a precise fashion. Behind, the big drystone ensemble eventually merges with the surrounding wall of cut stone.

4.7
Carlo Scarpa
BRION FAMILY CEMETERY
S. Vito, Italy
1973
for the Brion family

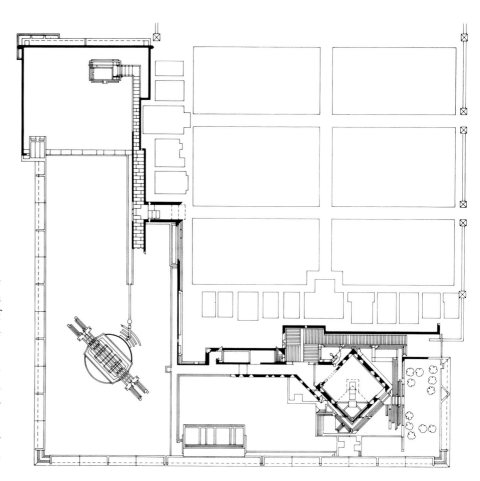

Carlo Scarpa was asked by the industrialist Giuseppe Brion to design the Brion cemetery and the tombs for him and his wife. The site was an L-shaped plot of land wrapped around the north-east corner of the local cemetery in the village of S. Vito, near Treviso. It is a traditional Italian cemetery, its plots and mausoleums arranged in a grid pattern with a central aisle on the axis of the long approach avenue bordered by cypress, the traditional trees of death.

The entrance to the walled Brion cemetery terminates this axis with a propylaeum, a board-marked

(*Opposite, top*) Plan of the Brion family cemetery wrapped around the corner of the local cemetery. The main entrance is off the old cemetery and leads to the cloister which runs north to the bog pool, south to the tomb, and round the corner to the chapel and a secondary entrance at the bottom right. The building at the lower centre is for relatives' tombs.

(*Left*) The sarcophagi of Brion and his wife, with the step motif carved into the ends, lean gently towards each other under the low concrete arch of the vault.

concrete portal festooned with ivy and overhung by the fronds of a weeping willow (the name of the plant and its connotations are the same in Italian). For the visitor on a pilgrimage, the local cemetery in a sense acts as a visual preliminary to the sacred place of the Brions. Inside the dark portal the visitor is confronted with a set of steps leading up to a transverse cloister. A glimpse of the distant ivy-covered inward-canting boundary wall and the mountains beyond is visible through a pair of inter-twined circles cut out of the concrete wall. It is the first of these motifs to be found throughout the landscape. Superficially it has something to do with traditional Chinese moon-gates. But there are other resonances: the interconnected circles in most cases have coloured rims, one blue, the other pink, refer-ences to male and female, sun and moon or perhaps lay and sacred love – and possibly all three. Later the visitor discovers the Brion tomb set in a circular depression, the stone sarcophagi of Brion and his wife gently canted towards each other under a curved canopy. And the circular motif, sometimes intertwined, sometimes connected and sometimes alone, appears under the surface of water, cut into other walls or terminating a channel of water.

The architectural elements of almost the whole of the landscape are in carefully designed board-marked concrete, sometimes inlaid with mosaic and often formed into a pattern of stepped layers. In the

(*Above*) The motif of entwined circles recurs throughout the design.

(*Opposite*) A view from the south of the plant-decked curve of the Brion tomb, with the canted perimeter wall behind and the end of the cloister to the right, the pool beyond.

155

short transverse cloister at the top of the stairs there is a choice of going to left or right. To the left is a view over the lawn to the Brion tomb, set diagonally in the corner of the enclosed landscape. It is formed from a pair of massive arched, doubled concrete beams spanning the depression containing the sarcophagi and springing from complicated stepped bastions on either side. A thin curving concrete canopy slung underneath the beams protects the sarcophagi; the whole ensemble is covered with climbing plants.

The tomb is the pivot of a right-angle change of direction, left to the cloisters leading to the chapel around the corner, and beyond to the secondary entrance, used primarily for burial services. By this secondary entrance is a plot for the burial of priests and back towards the tomb against the north wall is a structure which shelters memorial tablets for members of the family. The surrounding concrete wall is inclined inwards over the Brion cemetery, creating a heightened sense of enclosure from the surrounding fields but allowing a view of the distant mountains beyond.

If the visitor at the top of the stairs turns right down the cloister, he is confronted with a view of the square pool forming the south end of the cemetery. The way is blocked by a sheet of glass which has to be pushed down through a slit in the pavement. Beyond, the cloister opens up; the paving continues over the water at the edge of the pool and turns left on to the podium of a pavilion in the water.

The pool is enclosed on three sides by a concrete wall with a thin embedded line of mosaic tiles. A low edging separates it from the lawn. The end of the inward-sloping boundary wall hangs over one corner, transformed by adding another section of wall into a V-shaped planter half closed with a detail deploying the stepped layer theme. The pool contains three major elements: a square with projections on two sides and a polygon with a similar projection from it, both of which are only a few inches above water level. The polygon is filled with flowering plants and the centre of the mosaic inlaid square with gravel. The third element is the pavilion, actually a concrete podium with a timber and metal hood, rather like a *baldacchino* or helmet, suspended a foot above water level by slender bronze supports. It has a narrow slit in the north side. Inside the 'helmet' the only view possible is directly across the lawn to the Brion tomb. When the water is clear it becomes apparent that Scarpa has installed a number of concrete drums a few inches below water-level, some for water-plants, one intersecting pair repeating the primary symbol of the cemetery.

The pool is connected to the tomb by a water channel from its north-west corner running along the outside of the cloister under a set of cables stretched across the lawn to the boundary wall. It narrows beyond the north end of the cloister, to terminate in a small open drum beyond which is another drum set at the edge of the curving grass

steps leading down to the tomb. Here, possibly, is a repetition of the paired circle theme – in this case separated and connected only by a thin concrete spine. Built into the stairs but on the diagonal axis of the tomb is another concrete sculptural feature incorporating another smaller drum.

The Brion cemetery landscape is rich with symbolism, although Scarpa himself was never explicit about it. The buildings and decorative elements are believed to be based on the numbers 11 and 5.5: Carlo Scarpa's name has 11 letters. The underwater details, circles, steps and stepped layers are not immediately obvious, seen through the distorting veil of the water's surface, in some seasons clouded, in others mysteriously black. The immediate associations are to do with the waters of contemplation, with Lethe, the river of death, and with the existence of another world on, as it were, the other side of the veil. The channel between the tomb and the pool is, enigmatically, level: it may be that the three small drums are a reference to the water of life feeding the main pool, or, given the fact that water cannot flow between the three (there is no direct connection between them), that the water from the main pool symbolically disappears at the tomb. Rich symbolism is rarely explicit.

(*Left*) A view south from the hooded pavilion of the mosaic inlaid shape, one of a number in the pool or just below its surface; beyond are the doubled wires stretched low over the lawn, the canted perimeter wall and the low-slung vault.

(*Above*) The termination of the canted perimeter wall over the pool, which is enclosed by vertical walls. Scarpa has solved the problem of dealing with the conjunction of a vertical and an angled surface by mirroring the slope and using the resulting V-shape to serve as a hanging planter.

The function of the pool pavilion is resonant of Zen thinking; its only possible function is to provide a single channelled view of the tomb, perhaps to concentrate contemplation on the life of Brion or the larger mysteries of life and death. As one commentator has said, Scarpa's design 'must have originated from a deep understanding of ancient art, a meeting which . . . entrusts its message to the synthesis between visual image, physical matter and conceptual and executive techniques'.

Around the corner, on the north side of the cemetery, is a lawn set at a lower level and the square chapel set diagonally in a square pool. The pool edge has a number of sculptural details, mostly in the form of stepped layers formed from concrete, which are deliberately located below the surface of the water. This in a sense is the secondary, more functional part of the cemetery, with the priests' burial-ground and the family chapel. Scarpa himself is buried at the corner of the L, but outside the wall, in the village cemetery.

(*Above*) The hooded pavilion in the square pool at the north of the cemetery. From a sitting position, it is possible to view the main sweep of the landscape. Standing up, the visitor has a view only through a vertical slit in the right-hand side of the hood.

(*Left*) The steps down into the pool.

(*Opposite*) A detail of the insubstantial steel structural support for the hood and the step motif – here as elsewhere disappearing below the surface of the water.

5 THE SUBJECTIVE VISION

In many ways landscape design has hitherto been pri-marily about the modification of existing topographies. But the new landscape is as much as anything to do with ideas, visions, models of a better or more intriguing environment. Some of these designs are visions, never particularly intended to be built. Emilio Ambasz's Folly belongs, in spirit at least, to the long tradition of follies, secret places for the designer to act out his private fantasies; Van Valkenburgh's Eudoxia is a delicate exercise in answering the problem of flowers in landscape design. Both of these are only partly private, for they were designed for public themed exhibitions. More explicit is Bunschoten's Spinoza's Garden, both a model of a new town and a gallery installation representing the extraordinary qualities of the Dutch polders, reclaimed from an inimical ocean. Andrew Mahaddie's extraordinary, visionary scheme for the British new town of Milton Keynes combines an eclectic collection of references and forms, from the elements of prehistoric symbolism through to the most recent technological advances in building products, especially glass. Ian Hamilton Finlay's Little Sparta is a private/public landscape which has evolved into a didactic expression of the failings of the relationship between art and the public realm as he sees it. Three designs which share a common interest in the Zen qualities of Japanese landscape design, Zimmerman's Terrain at Chicago, Murase's Aichi Green Centre in Japan and Noguchi's Scenario in California, represent a private vision which happens to work in a public context.

The California Scenario, Costa Mesa, USA.

SPINOZA'S GARDEN

1985

for the Architecture Biennale, Netherlands

This scheme is an installation now owned by the Netherlands Architecture Museum and originally designed for the 1985 Architecture Biennale. The name derives from Bunschoten's preoccupation at the time with a great age of Dutch intellectual and artistic flowering. Bunschoten cites Heinrich Heine's characterization of Spinoza as a 'forest of lofty thoughts whose flowering tops sway while the immovable trunks are rooted in the eternal earth'. But the main theme behind it was the problem of creating new lands in the polders and in particular the way in which conventional planners had dealt with the new polder city of Almere. There were also references to the tiled surfaces of the old Berlage Exchange in which the biennale was held, and to more general issues about perception, contemplation, change and order. The only programmed constraint was that the work had to be capable of being dismantled for transport.

It consists of a hollow cube clad in coloured semi-translucent porcelain tiles set adjacent to a grid of 120 wooden cubes on which are set in three groups a variety of ceramic objects. The first set are cubic in shape in a greyish blue-green glaze with hollows of varying shapes crackle-glazed in a turquoise hue. Along the grid the cubes soon become plain earthenware, fragmented, with wires sprouting through them, and the final group is of porcelain shapes reminiscent of alchemical vessels. Each of the wire reeds is bifurcated at some point along its curving length.

Although it is designated a viewing-room it is possible to see into and out of the adjacent ceramic-clad cube only through small apertures in the walls or from the balcony of the Exchange above. It is a wooden structure lined on both sides with a grid of deep-ochre-glazed translucent porcelain tiles, some of which have been cut and some partly painted. Between the two sides Bunschoten installed curved lines of lighting which form a secondary pattern and create the feeling of a glowing furnace on the inside.

(***Above***) Two details of the enigmatic objects, perhaps alchemical in nature, among the steel reeds.

(***Right***) The installation as it was arranged for the Architecture Biennale in 1985. In the foreground is the base layer of wooden cubes with their ceramic shapes and steel 'reeds'. Behind is the ceramic-clad 'viewing room'.

(*Left*) The gradual disintegration of the clear hollow cubic shapes, with occasional fragments representing the detritus found when polders are drained.

(*Above*) The glazed wall of the viewing room, with glazed porcelain tiles fired by Bunschoten, some of them cut and some painted. The inner wall is lined with the same kind of tiling.

(*Right*) A view from the balcony of the famous Berlage Exchange. From the left the orthogonal quality of the glazed earthenware shapes is gradually transmuted, into forms more symbolic of the cracked earth of a dehydrating polder and then into objects of increasing delicacy, not only of form but of manufacture: the last objects are porcelain. In the same way there is a gradual change in the frequency of the steel reeds, which are bifurcated at some point along their length.

(*Opposite and right*)
Details of the reeds, some of them cluttered with symbolic detritus, growing from a collection of increasingly purposeful shapes reflecting Bunschoten's preoccupation at the time with the great age of Dutch intellectual flowering.

Here fragments of a sphere are suspended by wires which project through the walls rather like hairs and can be manipulated. The fragments are made from fibre-glass lined with mosaic.

There are some direct references to the main theme of the polders: the increasingly fragmented earthenware cubes relate to the cracked clay surface of a polder when it has begun to dry out, the steel reeds are a reference to the reeds which are normally seeded by aircraft to help the dehydration of the polders, and the fragmented sphere in the viewing-room furnace has perhaps to do with the cosmic quality of Spinoza's thought. In addition, the plan of the design actually fits into the central area of the plan of Almere, which at the time had not been completed. And Bunschoten used glazed ceramics as an acknowledgement of the dramatic ceramics of Berlage's Exchange interior. Direct references are of almost incidental importance, for Spinoza's Garden is, as Bunschoten describes it, in a sense a meta-

physical 1:500 scale topological model, an archaeology of what might have been there. Its function is less to do with specific realities than with other patterns and systems of relationships to which the model refers.

Bunschoten describes the creation of a polder after it has been dyked and pumped out. 'A world of silt remains – wet, uneven, punctuated by drowned, sunken objects such as ships or planes with their contents scattered around them. Reeds are sown from the air, which soon form a sea of swaying tops . . . The newly exposed objects disappear again among the stems of the reeds and wild flowers. Large cracks appear in the ground, insects arrive, birds begin to nest. The urban development which follows is a sad example of fast internal colonization.' Spinoza's Garden is, then, at the same time a critique of the banality of contemporary planning, which ignores the almost alchemical transmutation involved in making new lands.

5.2
Emilio Ambasz

EMILIO'S FOLLY: MAN IS AN ISLAND
1983

for the Castelli Gallery, New York, exhibition
Follies *organized by Barbara Jakobson*

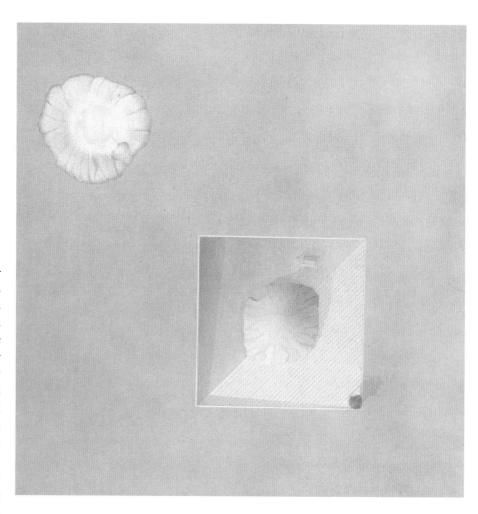

Designed at the request of Leo Castelli for an exhibition, *Follies*, at his New York gallery, this dream landscape came, explains Emilio Ambasz, as an image, 'fully fledged, clear and irreducible like a vision'. The site is thought of as a fertile plain of more than 8 hectares/20 acres somewhere in Texas or maybe Argentina. In the middle of this large grassy plain is a big, square, sunken courtyard bisected diagonally, one half water, the other a set of terraced earth steps leading down 4 metres/14 ft in a big sloping triangle from the corner to the water's edge. The entrance is marked by a three-legged structure, rather like a *baldacchino*, with a lemon tree planted in its roof. In the centre, half in the water, half on the terraced land, is a rock mass resembling a mountain. A domed chamber with a diagonal shaft pointing to the sky has been carved from its centre with a coved shore accessible only by water through the mountain's entrance.

Ambasz wished to move across the water by means of a barge, made from logs with a primitive hut on top which has a thatched roof and square-sectioned wooden columns. It is moved around the pool with a long pole – into the mountain grotto or over to the arcades on the far sides of the triangular pool. These arcades form an L in plan lining the two far sides of the pool, and support the overburden of soil above. Set back behind them is an undulating wall with openings into hidden alcoves.

Here, in his vision, Ambasz began to store things, piling childhood toys and memorabilia into each alcove until it was full and proceeding clockwise to the next one, which was used for remembrances from his military service and his uniform. 'I became fond of traversing the water basin once in a while to dress up in it, to make sure that I had not put on too much weight.'

In his dream, storing things became an almost compulsive activity and Ambasz found himself developing techniques for stacking in the seemingly insatiable alcoves, discovering that stored objects had shrunk or collapsed.

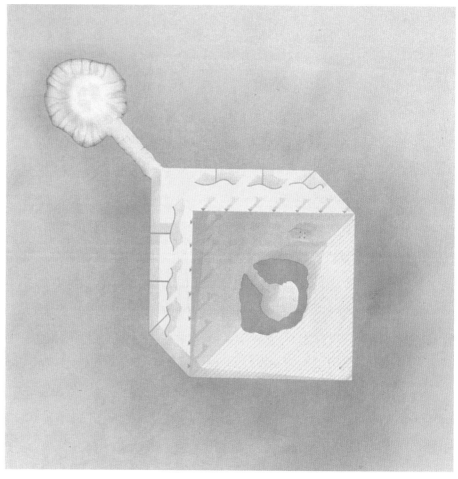

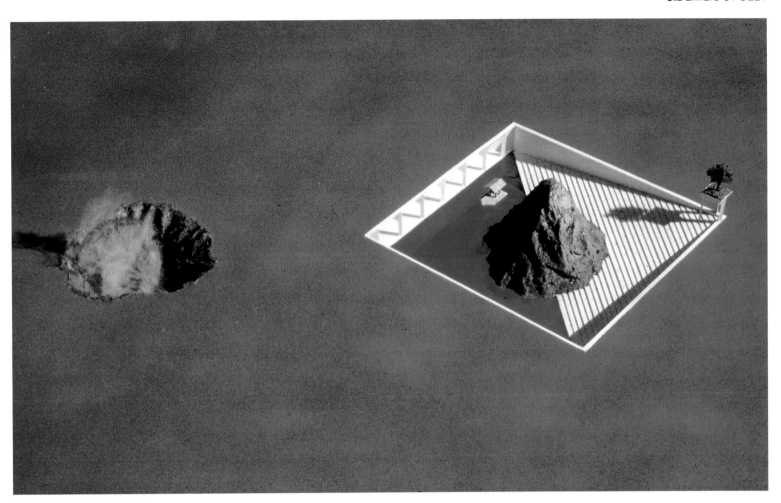

(*Opposite*) The ground-level plan (*top*): the mist-filled crater (*top left*), the triangular lake with a small hollow mountain half in the lake, half growing out of the terraced triangle leading down from the entrance. (*Below*) The subterranean plan.

The alcove at the corner of the arcade is missing. It is the entrance to an underground tunnel leading to the inner side of a crater-like depression in the ground, swathed with mist which always produces a rainbow. All that is visible from the plain outside is the rainbow in the mist, the top of the mountain and the surreal entrance *baldacchino* with its lemon tree unexpectedly rooted in the air.

Ambasz offers no particular rationalization for his dream landscape; he notes only that the structure is in reinforced concrete covered with earth and that the mist machines would be from MEE Fogging Devices of Pasadena, California. Whatever the explanation, the dreaming, de Chirico-like stereometry of the scheme is in a sense an idealization of much of Ambasz's architectural and landscape design, which has been characterized by buildings, usually of much more extensive scale than this, built beneath undulating land-forms, their lighting and entrances created by arbitrary slices and crevasses across the new topography. Like the best traditional follies, this is a small-scale synthesis of particular representational designs with the required added twist of enigma and mystery, obsessiveness and great beauty.

(*Top*) The mountain in the middle of the diamond-shaped, half-water-filled depression has a cave which is accessible by a thatched barge. It is also used to take Ambasz to the underground cloister surrounding the two leftmost sides of the depression, at whose apex an underground tunnel leads to the mist-filled pit.

(*Above*) From the imaginary plain, all that is visible is the entrance, under a tree planted atop a canopy held up by three columns, the top of the steep mountain and wisps of mist marking the presence of the crater.

5.3
Ian Hamilton Finlay
LITTLE SPARTA
nr Dunsyre, Scotland
1967 to date

(*Left*) The Little Sparta landscape: Scottish moorland with the gate at which Hamilton Finlay and his supporters staged their defiance of local rating officials.

Little Sparta is an allusive poet's landscape created by the Scottish artist Ian Hamilton Finlay for himself in a bleak moorland setting 40 kilometres/25 miles south-west of Edinburgh. It is a personal landscape whose themes have changed over the years in the direction of a celebration of neo-classicism. But it has always been a landscape in which works of art, inscriptions, planting and applied architectural features form an aesthetic network.

It is a landscape which is to some extent in the uniquely British tradition of the eighteenth-century *ferme ornée* of Shenstone's Leasowes and Hamilton's Painshill, both small-scale landscapes designed over a period of time by their owners – on shoestrings – and perhaps, too, it owes something to Clough Williams Ellis's twentieth-century version of an Italian town at Portmeirion. In addition, it is a landscape which has literally to be read, partly in the way eighteenth-century English landscapes such as Stourhead were designed to be read as a series of scenes from the painter Claude le Lorrain and the poet Virgil – and read in the sense of reading significant inscriptions on architectural features of those gardens. In Hamilton Finlay's case the inscriptions invariably have a double or hidden meaning. Thus one such, *Bring back the Birch*, is set in a grove of young birch trees. Cultures unfamiliar with British irony have sometimes taken this kind of thing literally, and he lost a major commission in France because of it.

As at Stowe, there is also a political dimension, for he has had long battles both with local building-tax bureaucrats and against the prevailing secular cultural ethos, which he has referred to with a nod at the French Revolution as the 'Secular Terror'.

The landscape is arranged around a small single-storey stone farm compound, itself loosely grouped around a large pool. To the east is a wood. Beyond the house to the south is a group of small semi-formal gardens and to the north three ponds; one, named Lochan Eck (Eck is the Scottish diminutive of Alexander, the name of Hamilton Finlay's son), is large enough to sail small boats on. Beyond is the treeless moorland and on one side farmland.

The small gardens to the south by the entrance gate are each self-contained and surrounded by shoulder-height shrubs and flowers on trellises. On axis with the front of the farmhouse is a sloping path leading to a sunken garden of rock plants and camomile, where there is a sundial and works of sculpture, including weathercocks, all embodying a poetic analogy between the elements and the theme which has been established. Diamond-shaped cast concrete paving-stones in the grass leading to the garden are inscribed, some with the names of different boat types, others with the names of boats: an early theme at Little Sparta was the contrast between garden and sea, between what is feasible and the unconquerable.

The Roman garden to the south-west surrounded by a small grove of cypresses is a formal paved area, its entrance marked by a Palladian column; it is set with potted plants, stone bird-baths and bird-tables

(*Below*) The arrangement of Little Sparta in the late 1980s: the entrance gate (*bottom left*), the small formal gardens adjacent and then the farmyard complex surrounding the inner lake. At the top right is the largest water, Lochan Eck.

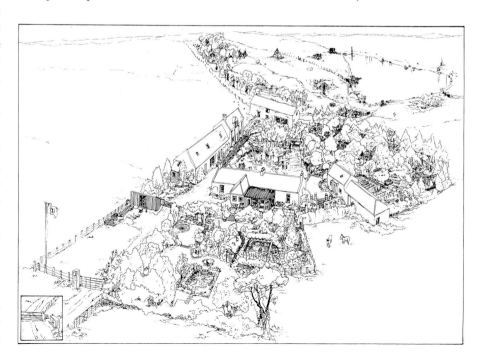

Two painterly
references, to Albrecht
Dürer (*top*) and to
Claude (*below*): the
tablet is inscribed with
Dürer's monogram and
the inscription on the
obelisk beside the upper
pool reads *Il Riposo di
Claudio*.

based on modern warships (coincidentally Italian Renaissance gardens sometimes included stone ships). The carved stone prow of the USS Nautilus emerges from a stand of firs, perhaps a metaphor for the ocean. Elsewhere are inscribed wooden posts with false shadows of brick set in the adjacent turf, a reference to the relatively cloudy skies of this part of Britain. The most obvious neo-classical references are the fallen and upright, complete and broken classical columns, capitals, brackets and obelisks variously scattered around the grass, by the side of pools and among the trees.

In the farm courtyard on a small island in the pond is the largest of the warship bird-tables, in the form of

Two painterly references, to Albrecht Dürer (*top*) and to Claude (*below*): the tablet is inscribed with Dürer's monogram and the inscription on the obelisk beside the upper pool reads *Il Riposo di Claudio*.

a stone aircraft-carrier mounted on a polished stone column reflected in the water. Beyond the lake to the north is a stone representation of a nuclear submarine sail. Nearby in the farm courtyard, hanging on a tree, is a wooden slab inscribed in reverse with the names of Angelica and Medoro, the lovers in Ariosto's *Orlando Furioso* who carved their names on a tree. The inscription can only be read properly when reflected in the water. Not far away is a group of irises, reeds and other planting which closely follows the composition of Albrecht Dürer's watercolour *The Great Piece of Turf*. Dürer's monogram is inscribed on a stone tablet, in a sense signing the composition.

Hamilton Finlay has added vestigial Corinthian pilasters to one of the old farm buildings and added the inscription in large Roman lettering *TO APOLLO HIS MUSIC HIS MISSILES HIS MUSES*. Opposite is another outbuilding transformed by the addition of a rough stone portico into the Temple of Baucis and Philemon.

Moving out of the densely planted area, the visitor crosses a concrete bridge traversing the burn which connects the various areas of water. It is inscribed in very large letters *CLAVDI*, an intimation of the somewhat Claudian landscape beyond. The banks of the stream below are planted with rhubarb.

In the large lake, Lochan Eck, is a small wooded island dedicated to Rousseau with a stone tablet standing on four columns. It is a reference to the tomb of Rousseau at Ermenonville, the great estate where the Marquis de Giradin looked after the French philosopher in his last years. In another garden is a ceramic basket of cherries set on a column, a reference to an episode in Rousseau's *Confessions*. At the edge of the lochan is a stone sculpture in the form of a nuclear submarine sail and some distance away are 11 stones inscribed with *THE PRESENT ORDER IS THE DISORDER OF THE FUTURE – SAINT JUST*. To the west is the upper pool where inscriptions and architectural fragments reinforce the literary and artistic theme of incongruous and unexpected juxtapositions, whose ultimate function is to raise questions in the visitor's mind about the conventional stance of contemporary thinking.

(*Left*) The inscription on the cut stones laid out on the rough turf at the north-west edge of Little Sparta is a quotation from Saint-Just. It is a commentary obliquely supporting his stance on the relationship between art and the public realm.

(*Top*) A stone-carved representation of the sail of a nuclear submarine, appositely reflected in the water in front of it, dates from an earlier phase in the iconography of the landscape.

5.4
Robert Murase

AICHI GREEN CENTRE

Nishi-Kamo, Japan
1974
for Aichi Prefecture

The American landscape architect Robert Murase designed this two-hectare/five-acre entry landscape for the Green Centre, a botanical garden and conference centre master-planned by Akira Okazaki and Makoto Nakamura for the Aichi Prefecture. It is an hour's drive from Nagoya, the nearest large city, and is set in an area of gently rolling hills and conifer forests.

The Aichi prefectural government wanted a transition landscape from the nearby arterial road via a car and bus park to the centre's facilities. It was to incorporate rest-rooms, arbours and an information facility. Its primary function was to provide a place where visitors could orientate themselves on arrival before going in the direction of the conference centre, Japanese garden and botanical garden. Japanese tourists normally travel in large groups; Murase therefore had the problem of designing a large space which also worked visually when it was empty. His brief was to create a focused space with the qualities of quietness and serenity – the ambience of a traditional Japanese garden.

The site is just north of an arterial road, so Murase lowered the main plaza area to provide acoustic shielding from traffic noise. The ground-level car park is a long *cul-de-sac* on the north with access from outside by a slip-road running along the west of the site. Visitors walk back south, down three wide flights of steps or a ramp on one side planted with broad-leaf deciduous trees, to a paved area. There is an alternative entrance from a tunnel under the slip-road to the east. Here the visitor has the option of going on to the public facilities, east to the botanic garden or down a set of shallow terraces to the core of the design, a roughly square paved area sloping gently down to a central pool.

The two paved areas are surrounded by curving low stone walls with a mixture of conifer and zelkova tree planting and rhododendrons and azaleas

(*Left*) Plan and lateral section of the centre, with the main access road (*top*), car parking (*right*) and pool (*left*).

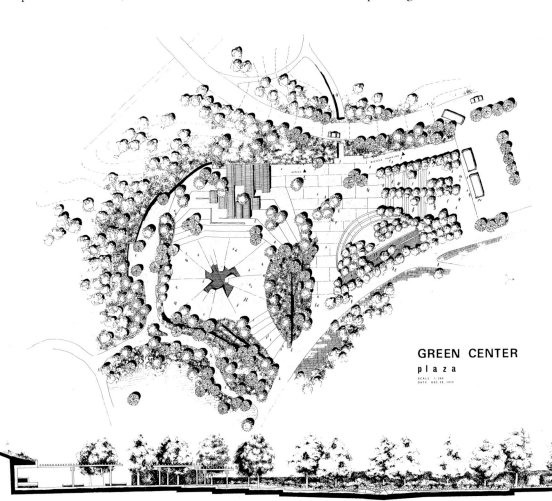

GREEN CENTER
plaza
SCALE 1:300
DATE DEC 28, 1973

(*Above and right*) Long, dry, enigmatic channels are cut through the paving from the surrounding walls into the central pool and its geological formations. They contribute to the feeling that the paved, slightly dished area has been modified by some great force and left to regain its tranquillity.

behind them. The pool area is organized as a group of paved segments of cut granite separated by shallow channels which converge on the pool, terminating with large, very carefully placed pieces of fractured granite which form its edges. This can be viewed as a central pool with islands of stone emerging from its edges as if they have been forced up fragmented from the earth's surface, breaking through the organized pattern of the paving. They are intended to symbolize the Japanese people's island culture and their fragile volcanic environment. At the same time they work as pieces of sculpture, arranged in an abstract geometric form which is intended to give an evocative emotional experience for people standing or sitting in the space.

Murase points out that his intention was not to capture the energy of the space by the use of water. It is the stones which do this. Their positioning was critical: Murase made extensive use of a clay model to develop their detailed arrangement and form. A plaster copy was given to the stonemasons to aid their understanding of the complex construction drawings.

There was a problem with a natural spring at the foot of one of the low hills by the car-parking area. In keeping with the whole design, Murase accepted its existence and allowed it to emerge naturally into an area of wetland planting material around and below the source. This small wetland ensemble became incorporated into the botanical garden.

Murase is happy to be thought of as a designer of Japanese gardens. For him they reflect an attitude and understanding of nature which is spiritual and compassionate. Their basic elements are carefully selected and stones are placed as groups or as single features arranged to create tension or serenity. The stones at the Green Centre's pool are a deliberate attempt to create a connection to the modus of traditional Japanese landscape. His concern is primarily with the detailed qualities of the materials of his landscape – the sound of water, stillness, the way light is reflected and the patterns it forms, the texture and mystery of stone – qualities which create an almost primordial relationship between the landscape and its viewer.

(*Above*) Long stones are tilted up around the perimeter of the pool to create a powerful sense of primordial geological action which has left a still pool in the centre of the eruption. The stone walls and their backing planting create a sense of stillness.

(*Opposite*) The transition between cut paving and the 'eruptions' around the perimeter of the pool.

5.5
SITE

THE FOUR CONTINENTS BRIDGE

Hiroshima, Japan
1989
for Sea & Island Expo Association

The environmental design and architecture group SITE was asked to design a bridge as the centrepiece for the Hiroshima Sea and Island Expo during the summer and autumn of 1989. The director of the Expo had seen SITE's Highway '86 Processional, an undulating four-lane roadway crowded with every type of transportation, at the Vancouver Expo. SITE's brief was that the bridge should symbolize the theme of the Expo: the connections between land, sea and people.

The bridge linked two major areas of the Expo site separated by an artificial lagoon. SITE decided to invert the normal circumstances of bridges in traditional landscapes which simply carry people from one part of the landscape to another. This bridge was itself to form a landscape. A further inversion was the fact that bridges normally passed over water. Here water was an essential part of the bridge ensemble. It is an embracing and inversion of the concept of 'bridge'. There are some historical precedents, such as the turf bridge at the eighteenth-century Stourhead, the Ponte Vecchio in Florence and perhaps the original London Bridge, on which people had built

houses and shops as extensions of the medieval city; and the traditional Japanese practice of edging bridges with mosses and small plants.

At Hiroshima, Joshua Weinstein, James Wines and Glen Coborn of SITE, working with the landscape architect Signe Nielson, developed a design which was intended also to symbolize man's eternal responsibility to help preserve nature and its resources. The bridge has two walkways on either side of four set-piece landscapes representing Africa, Asia, the Americas and Europe: they are planted with vegetation and trees which are typical of the four continents. They include date and fan palms and African aloe for Africa, Abyssinian banana, sago palms and Japanese aralia for Asia, Joshua trees, cactus, creosote and rye grass for the Americas, birch, pine, phlox, daisies and Corsican mint for Europe. The planting is a mixture of trees, shrubs and ground-cover plants.

The bridge is a low arch, reminiscent of traditional Japanese bridges, but here in steel with a concrete deck. The enclosures on the bridge are built in glass framed with steel tubes. They include the entrances, the enclosures for the four symbolic landscapes, glass-roofed walk-throughs between them and a spine wall which runs the full length of the bridge, splitting it in half. One side of the bridge represents land environments, the other those of the sea.

On the land side the sloping edge of the bridge is heavily planted out with low shrubs, a basic planting of trumpet creepers, red climbing geranium, Japanese ivy and grape vines interspersed with plants of the four continents. On the other side of the walkway, handrail-height glass walls contain the layers of earth in which the representative continental planting is set, in a very large-scale version of a terrarium. The earth ramps up irregularly to head height at the back against the central dividing glass wall, so that

(*Opposite*) **The 'land' side of the bridge, with the first of the continental landscapes on the left. The low curve of the bridge belongs to a family of traditional Japanese bridge profiles. Here the edge is planted out with low shrubs, interspersed with plants representative of the four continents on the other side of the path.**

(*Left*) **Plan: the four divisions are for landscapes typical of Africa, Asia, the Americas and Europe. The middle spine divides the terraria from the wet, largely rocky landscapes on the sea side of the bridge.**

(*Opposite below*) **The terrarium on the 'sea' side of the bridge, a slice through the earth. It is enclosed by glass framed in steel tubing whose upper rail trickles water down the glass to the rockscape below.**

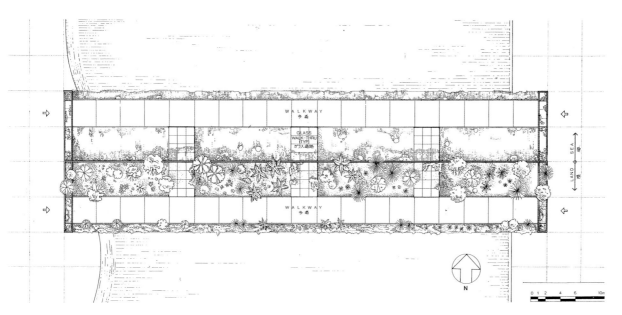

people crossing through the three glazed tunnels to the sea environment side can observe the changing substructure of the symbolic gardens and the small animal and insect life, which quickly developed habitats against the glass. They have in a sense walked through an archaeological dig, a slice in the earth, emerging to find that they have become part of a water environment. The dividing glass wall through which they have come is irrigated from the top, so that the wall is not so much glass, more a vertical sheet of water draining into four rock water-gardens which mirror the symbolic gardens on the other side. They represent the wet-edge habitat between sea and land. The water drains from here under the raised walkway, a bridge as it were on a bridge, and emerges on the other side as a pluming waterfall running the full length of this side of the bridge. The

glazed entrances which serve to contain the bridge landscape are also irrigated with water sprays – as in the main spine wall, where they are fixed to the underside of the structural tube which also acts as a water-pipe.

The Four Continents bridge existed only for the six months of the Expo; it was disassembled and the structural steel returned to the stockholder from whom it had been leased: a neat piece of Japanese lateral thinking. Filling the terrariums with massive amounts of earth would have created enormous structural loads on both the sub-frame and the glass: the earth was actually a relatively thin layer over styrene foam blocks, dug out in the higher levels to take the roots of trees.

SITE's landscape is to do with taking popular and often very simple concepts and turning them round, inverting their expected meaning, changing their scale dramatically, and layering elements on each other and at the same time creating visual environments which are pleasurable for curious and ordinary people. And people form the third vital element of the Expo theme. In the end the organizers changed the name from 'four continents' to 'the bridge which connects the world'.

(*Top*) The exit from the sea side of the bridge, the water garden in the foreground and the water-flushed glass walls across the end. The water appears to drain under the walkway and spray over the edge into the lake.

(*Right*) The 'sea' side of the bridge gives the impression less of a bridge than of a low, wide waterfall, with the walkway a narrow bridge over the water trickling down the long glass wall across the wet landscapes in front. Bridges are not necessarily bridges.

5.6

Isamu Noguchi

CALIFORNIA SCENARIO

Costa Mesa, California
1983
for Henry T. Segerstrom

The site for Isamu Noguchi's California Scenario is a large suburban space in the Costa Mesa. It is bounded on two adjacent sides by tall mirror-glass office towers and on the other sides by the high blank stucco walls of car-parking buildings. In this flat, neutral, almost square space Noguchi disposed a number of elements, earth mounds, geometric and sculptural forms, some planting and a meandering water-course across the paved stone surface. Originally a sculptor, Noguchi has said, 'I like to think of gardens as sculpturing of space . . . A man may enter such a space: it is in scale with him; it is real. An empty space has no visual dimension . . . scale and meaning enter when some thoughtful object or line is introduced. That is why sculptures, or rather sculptural objects, create space. Their function is illusionist. The size and shape of each element is entirely relative to all the others and the given space. What may be incomplete as sculptural entities are of significance to the whole. Such sculpture is eliminative, it is neither this nor that but a thing in space that affects our consciousness . . . without content related

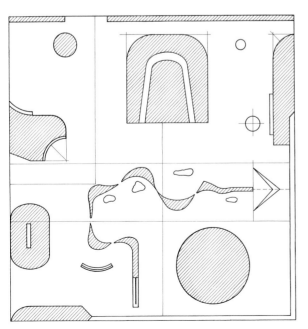

to or derived from anything exterior to its purpose – in effect subliminal. These sculptures I call a garden.'

The ground is paved mostly with very large, flat, irregular, pinkish stones which in one or two arbitrary cases are squared up. Here and there are single large boulders and a group of 15 large interlocking granite pieces forms a sculpture called *Spirit of the Lima Bean*, dedicated by Noguchi to his client, whose family since the early part of the century had farmed lima beans locally. A formal fountain called the Energy Fountain is a cone made up of squarish stones with a cylindrical jet at the top and an annular trough at the base to collect the water bouncing down. It is on the opposite side of the *mesa* and quite unconnected to the main water-course cut into the paving.

The water-course gushes out of a trough set between two freestanding triangular walls, runs around the courtyard, disappearing here and there

(*Far left*) **Schematic plan of California Scenario. Clockwise from the top left, the main features are: the Energy Fountain, the Forest Walk, a bed of redwoods, the circular Desert Land, the Water Source, Land Use with the *Monument to Development* and another redwood mound fronted by a curved seat.**

under the paving, and finally vanishes under a low pyramidal stone form. The water moves along its flat course enlivened by small jets embedded in the edges of the stream. On its way the thickness of the paving, visible at the edge of the stream, decreases – perhaps referring to the erosion of youth into old age.

There are five mounded areas. One, in the corner, cut off by the stream's course and equidistant from its source and conclusion, is called Desert Land. It is exactly circular, covered with sand and gravel and planted with cacti and desert species.

The grassy mound across the stream is designated Land Use and has a plain coffin-like granite slab entitled *Monument to Development* embedded in its top. The Forest Walk is a simple mound with a U-shaped path leading up to a seat. It has pines planted around its perimeter, and two other mounded areas are heavily planted with redwoods. This was the first

(*Left*) The Water Source is the origin for the landscape's main water, emerging from between two triangular cheek walls with the plain stucco wall of one of the car parks making a neutral background. The stream follows a course apparently cut in the paving. To the left is the beginning of the Desert Land area.

(*Left*) The irregular water-course reads as either a glacial stream, littered with detritus, whose banks have been undercut, or as a water-channel which has been revealed by ripping apart the stone paving in certain spots. The occasional solitary standing stones make an oblique reference to traditional Japanese stone gardens.

(*Opposite*) The Desert Land, an exactly circular gravel and sand mound, is sparsely planted with desert cacti. The triangular cheeks of the Water Source are adjacent: a symbolic contrast of desert extremes.

(*Above*) The Forest Walk surrounded by pines.

(*Left*) The severe formality of the geometric shapes of the Energy Fountain is modulated by the rough, square stones, which bounce the water cascading from the fountain in a constantly sparkling, moving cone shape.

time Noguchi had used plant materials in a way which would allow the design to change over time: the redwoods when first planted formed a miniature forest, but in half a decade will have changed out of all recognition.

One reading of this landscape is as a series of formal and regular shapes drawn on the flat in a seemingly arbitrary fashion and given names as a hint to some kind of possible narrative content. The individual boulders and the *Spirit of the Lima Bean* group make reference to Japanese rock gardens, and the flat irregular paving has resonances of the rock desert floor. But none of these things is necessarily particularly true. Noguchi has nevertheless created a powerful and mysterious image whose uncertainties of purpose are intended to evoke responses other than those of the conventional pleasure of experiencing landscape. He put it once that he wanted to create 'beautiful and disturbing gardens to awaken us to a new awareness of our solitude'.

5.7
Michael Van Valkenburgh
EUDOXIA
design for a new civic landscape

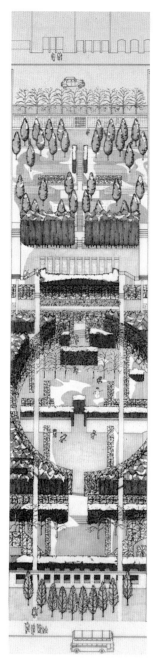
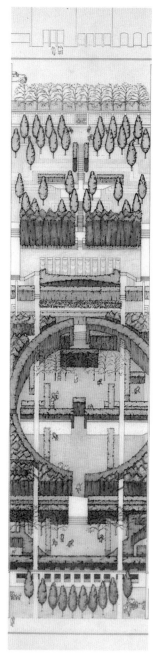
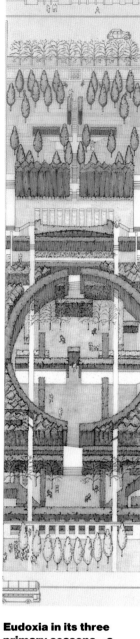

Eudoxia in its three primary seasons – a considered understanding of the importance of seasonality.

The landscape is intended for an urban site between two new three-storey buildings a full city block deep, facing the streets to north and south. The side buildings have continuous double-storey arcades running the full depth of each side of the site, so that the landscape is accessible from the sides as well as the two streets. At the south there are two entrances through a 3.5 metre/12-ft stuccoed screen wall set back from the pavement. In front is an arc of trees and behind a parallel evergreen hedge. Windows in the screen wall are repeated in square cut-outs in the hedge as are the two entrances on either side, providing views of the complex landscape beyond.

The design progresses north as a series of enclosed spaces or rooms with planting which has been chosen to create particular effects – fragrance, colour, texture, density, light, form – over the three growing seasons of the year. They are in most cases abstract geometric spaces linked by a path which is sometimes central, sometimes on two parallel routes at the side.

Through the south entrance hedge is an open space surrounded by hedges cut into a labyrinth of passages between the two side arcades linking the two buildings. Each individual hedge is composed of one plant species: evergreen or deciduous, some with unpruned tops, others clipped. A set of five wide steps leads down to a big circular space, offset from the landscape's centre-line and surrounded by a 5-metre/16-ft-high purple beech hedge. Because the circle is off-centre one side is clipped off by the structure of the east arcade. In this space is a series of hedges trimmed to prismatic forms, with an off-centre cross wall broken at three points reflecting the hedges behind. Beyond is a row of six deciduous trees in front of a short cross hedge and beyond that there are stairs leading out of the circle to a narrow cross room. Its north side is a long raised herbaceous border, with blue-flowered Siberian irises in season.

At either end of the border dog-leg stairs lead down to walkways overlooking a stone-surfaced water-court whose north side is faced with a 6-metre/20-ft hemlock hedge. The entrance to the water-court is from the north down a set of stairs in the middle of the hedge. The visitor is faced with a 7.5-metre/25-ft-high rock wall with stone pillars on each side, topped by a low, gently curving hedge. Eleven water trays cut into the ground empty into a long pool along the base of the rock face. The top of the wall is pierced by water-pipes which trickle or pour water down the rock. Cut deep into the ground, the water-court is isolated from the noise of the city beyond. There are recessed niches under the side walkways for quiet contemplation. In winter the water freezes, creating an irregular deep blue skin which reflects what sunlight reaches this north-facing wall.

A long axial flight of stairs leads north up a geometrically terraced slope planted with evergreen

190

The central section of Eudoxia, a great circle slightly offset from the centre line of the landscape with a cross hedge whose breaks reflect the hedges beyond. Behind (*top*) is the rock wall and its trickles of water which in winter turn to ice.

trees and framed with hedges. The columnar trees emphasize the steep change of level up to the north screen fence, lined on the street side by a formal row of deciduous trees.

This magical, formal landscape combines elements of private gardens, such as those of Lutyens, Jekyll and Vita Sackville West, but at a city scale and city level of complexity. Van Valkenburgh links his design strategy with the preoccupation of early twentieth-century modernism with geometric forms and spaces, proportion and dynamic balance rather than symmetry, and with Cubism and especially the paintings of Moholy-Nagy. Underneath is an essay of somewhat Platonic Formal character – art as the reflection of the true Form; here the landscape is seen as 'a scenography for contemporary life'.

5.8

Andrew Mahaddie

Design for

MILTON KEYNES CITY CENTRE PARK

Milton Keynes, Buckinghamshire, UK
1975

Milton Keynes was the last of the British new towns; it was created on a vast green field site in Buckinghamshire. It was also a notable departure from the townscape layouts of previous new towns, in that it was based on a grid defined by snaking roads. Individual developments took place in each of the grid-squares and were hidden by massive banks and heavy planting. The grid of the central area of the city, whose centrepiece was a great shopping building in the style of Mies van der Rohe, overlooked an adjacent grid-square of sweeping parkland. Andrew Mahaddie, a landscape designer with the city's development corporation, worked out a major design for the park.

The focal point of Mahaddie's landscape was a great truncated cone set on a low podium of the same formation. Access to it was directly from the belvedere, a low mound heavily planted with concentric rings of trees and reached from the city's shopping zone via a pedestrian bridge over one of the main city grid roads. From the top of the cone a long staircase led down to the next focal point, a vast circular pool, with a series of zigzag ramps from the skirting slope providing an easier alternative route. From the pool pedestrians either descended a narrow staircase to the bottom of a ravine or continued at ground level via a glass bridge over the ravine. This bridge ran across to a round green containing an inverted cone to an anechoic sound grotto, or in some versions of the design a round pond surrounded by seating decorated in a variety of geometric motifs, each making reference to an animal. Beyond that the path led to a children's play-castle and an earth promontory from which the remainder of the parkland, wild garden and sculpture park could be viewed. North of this prospect point a path led to the edge of a vast bowl for public performances and thence west to the belvedere and back to the shopping centre. Paths around the perimeter of the site provided access to the rolling parkland and sculpture park.

The design was founded in a set of heterogeneous ideas to do with prehistoric mysticism, together with an understanding of some of the more pleasurable aspects of Italian Renaissance garden design, some of the more austere aspects of neo-classicism and a hard-edged hi-tech element. For British traditional landscape designers at the time it represented an unwelcome intrusion on the soft-edged post-Picturesque principles on which they operated.

The mystical element is by no means fanciful. A group of the new-town designers were for a period heavily involved in exploring mysticism: such things as ley lines and primitive nature symbolism. They named the principal roads running alongside the adjacent shopping centre Avebury (after the megalithic site near Stonehenge), Silbury and Midsummer Boulevards, and reorientated them from their original alignment so that they caught the sun during the midsummer solstice. Mahaddie orientated his design on true north. The central cone itself is a conscious reference to one of Britain's most mysterious man-made earth-forms, Silbury Hill in Wiltshire. It also

(Above) **The great cone dominates the formal landscape. Stairs lead down to the big basin in the foreground. In Renaissance fashion alternative ramps zigzag down the cone's sloping base. The great basin has razor-sharp edges, and on a calm day would read as a great circular mirror. The catwalks take visitors inches above the surface of the water; on either side are what appear to be suspended horizontal strips of water, actually supported on tilted cantilevered glass slabs. The stairway in the main pool concourse leads down to the canyon below the glass bridge, whose approach handrails are at the centre bottom.**

(*Right*) The circular children's play area on the other side of the bridge.

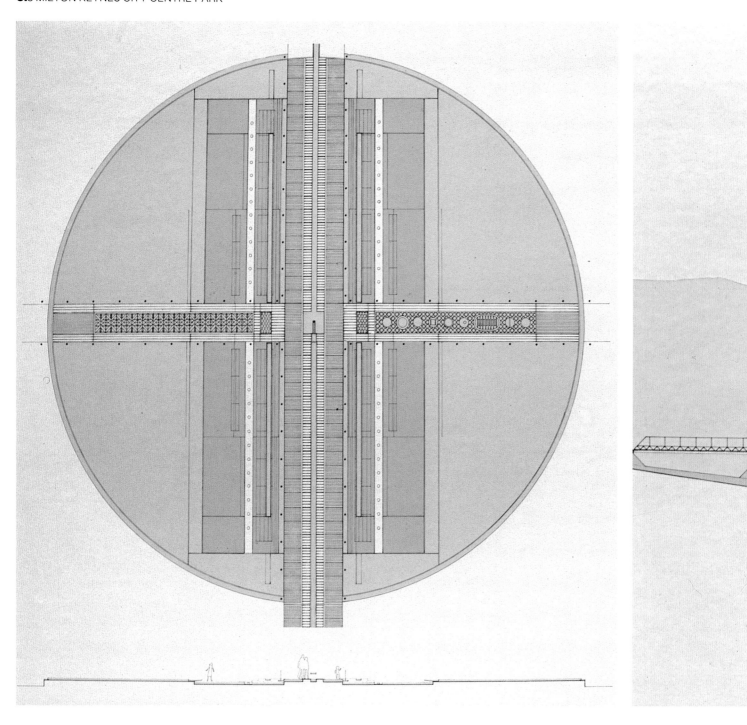

has an architectural precedent in the published designs of the late-eighteenth-century French neo-classical architect Ledoux, whose work was being rediscovered at the time. The steep range of steps from the flat platform on top down through a great sloping circular symbol is probably a reference to Mayan and Aztec temples. Randomly arranged bumps in the surrounding parkland make reference to prehistoric barrows.

In contrast, the zigzagging ramps on either side of the formal stairway down the lower reaches of the podium cone have a clear Italian source, as has the juxtaposition of the great circular tank at its foot: this is a pool which reads as a sheet of water without an apparent container; a gutter around the perimeter takes displaced water. The pool has two paths over it and a rectangular water carpet. The walkways are either solid blocks, the top face level with the surrounding water, with wide water-filled open joints, or they are suspended mesh grids, also laid almost submerged in the water. On the secondary path the paving takes a number of forms, including linked floating paving which undulates as it is walked on, paving-stones which, in the Renaissance manner, squirt a jet when they are walked on or which light up the path from beneath, hydraulically linked rise-and-sink paving pads, vibrating paving, bubble-inducing paving, zones of fog and mist jets, concealed underground lighting for the evening and adjoining cantilevered razor-edged pools which

(*Above left*) One of the designs for the great circular pool, its central section a water carpet with a cross axis deploying another set of somewhat Renaissance-inspired ambiguities: squirting, floating, vibrating, fog-inducing paving.

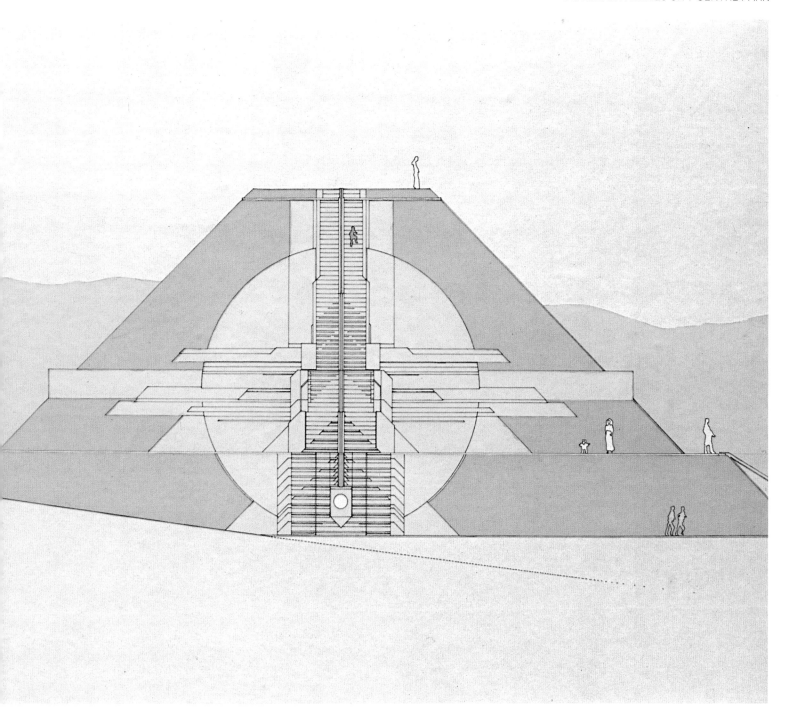

(*Above*) The great mound based on the conical form of Silbury Hill with its formal staircase.

appear to hang horizontal sheets of water over sections of the pool. All the materials here are hard-edged, glass, concrete or steel, with bright colours confined to narrow linear highlights in shallow recesses in the materials.

The design underwent a number of revisions and refinements but before a definitive scheme could be started, political, financial and aesthetic pressures forced it to be pulled from the new-town construction programme.

Whether based on mysticism, an attempt to relate to the mysterious forces of the earth, or not, the design demonstrated that it was possible to incorporate hard-edged geometric elements into a naturalistic landscape. Provided the relationship was understood

between certain pure Platonic geometric forms and the basic structure of nature, there was an additional internal consonance between the existing topography and the new building.

5.9
Elyn Zimmerman
TERRAIN, O'HARE INTERNATIONAL CENTER
Chicago
1987

for Hawthorn Realty Group and Melvin Simon & Associates

Hawthorn Realty asked the environmental artist Elyn Zimmerman to create a public plaza for their new headquarters in an airport periphery zone among a maze of highways, airline support facilities, car parks and undistinguished architecture. The 106 × 45-metre/350 × 150-ft site is surrounded by office buildings, with car-parking spaces in front reached from a private road around the landscape exiting to the busy airport highway on the east. The curved east end of the site follows the road. Zimmerman argued that conventional ideas about integrating architecture and landscape made no sense on this site because the buildings were set too far back behind the peripheral road. Her approach was to create an island, an evocative self-contained place.

She divided the site roughly into three. On the east is an undulating area planted with silver maples, perennials and heavy ground-cover in a naturalistic formation. Three paths drive west through this wood, with sitting-out spaces of a variety of sizes and two pools edged with rock and surrounded by water-margin plants. The undulating east edge of the

upper garden is bordered by large pieces of flat stone, below which are four undulating steps the width of the site leading down to the middle section. Each of these small terrace levels is in differently coloured stone. This middle section is around two metres/six feet below the level of the surrounding road and is entirely surfaced with square limestone pavers. Near the south-east corner is an irregular pool cut out of the paving which is dotted with 22 boulders, many of them well above head height, recalling both the Japanese tradition and, for European eyes, prehistoric standing stones. A narrow irregular channel cut in the pavers carries a small stream from the pool to the edge of the paving and down to a pool in the lower garden.

This lower eastern section is reached by four more terraced steps down to a flat gravel floor surrounded by a crescent-shaped berm planted with shrubs and wild flowers. It creates a visual barrier against the highway environment outside. The lower pool undercuts a section of the lower terrace and the water from the stone field pool disappears through a break at the edge of the paving and the steps in a tiny waterfall into the lower water-level. Stones of a slightly different character and shape are placed around the gravelled floor.

Zimmerman chose glacial erratics for the 26 stones in the middle stone field. They have been very carefully placed but are apparently arranged in a random pattern, found objects which themselves have been moved by glacial action from their original geological location to the point of discovery in the quarry. There they were useless for ordinary commercial purposes because of their geologically alien composition. The stones in the lower garden are paler and less megalithic in character, low enough to serve as seating by the lower pool.

Although there are stairs leading down from the peripheral road into the stone field there is a curious absence of axiality or of focus. The three spaces are different but Zimmerman has deliberately not given

(**Above**) Three paths wind through the wood and encircle the small pools; here there is space to sit.

(**Opposite**) At the eastern edge of the stone field the paving is terraced in several shallow layers. The arbitrary path of the water is cut into the paving and through the layers at the edge before falling into the pool in the lower zone. From the stone field the paving reads as the solid base for the massive standing stones, at the edge as an artificial, hard layer of stone.

(**Below left**) Plan of the Terrain, set in the middle of a small commercial office development. The main car access is from the left, off the main airport road system. The site slopes down from the left, and this slope is accommodated by Zimmerman's three levels.

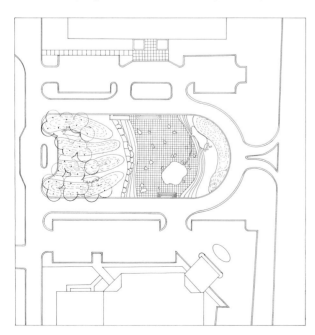

any one particular precedence. There are shade trees for people who want to sit around the upper pools, rocks to sit on round the pool of the lower garden and an enigmatic place to walk or sit on the upper terraced stairs in the stone field.

This central area is one of unequivocally hard, solid surfaces. Initially the precisely square limestone paving seems to have been laid hard on the ground – until the observer sees the edge of the pool and the meandering channel. Here it is clear that the paving is only an inch thick and overhangs the invisible, real perimeter of the water. There is a deliberate and faintly disturbing incongruity in having so precisely laid the paving, then studding it with wild rocks and

finally mechanically cutting sections of it out in order to create waterways. The result is that from the lower garden, where the terraced steps are partly undercut as well, the view is rather more of a thin, precise layer of surfacing which seems too insubstantial to bear the weight of the vast boulders on its surface.

The terrain can also be read as a section from an ancient landscape, with the stone field a metaphorical dried water-bed, one edge of which has been shifted down by geological action. A dark residual pool drains over its edge to a new pool surrounded by new vegetation. Meantime, on the flat river-bed, there remains the detritus of primordial natural forces.

6 RECONDITIONING NATURE

In some cases the problems of landscape design are extreme, as at Richard Haag's Gas Works Park, Seattle, on a site massively polluted by ugly industry. The long-term API design for Cergy Neuville's destructive sand-workings has continued during a period when the extractive industry ran a long phasing-out process. And, too, the Daniel Stewart design on a private estate on Long Island had to take notice of the greater littoral landscape of the Atlantic seaboard. At Wateridge, San Diego, Roger DeWeese has taken the banal semi-arid hillocky landscape and used water (very efficiently recycled) to create a landscape for commercial development. At Solana, Texas, Peter Walker has created an extensive commercial development landscape which makes reference to the agricultural and horticultural traditions of the area; at the same time it links the buildings with a comfortable mixture of the naturalistic and the formal landscape – the latter with deconstructivist tendencies. And Preben Jakobsen at Broadwater Park in the UK has made subtle alterations to both the topography and planting of this commercial setting.

Broadwater Park, Denham, Buckinghamshire, UK.

6.1
API

BASE DE PLEIN AIR ET LOISIRS

Cergy Neuville, Val d'Oise, France
1974 to date

for Syndicat Mixte d'Etude d'Aménagement et de Gestion de Base de Loisirs and L'Agence Foncière et Technique de la Région Parisienne

In the late 1960s Cergy New Town was established near the old town of Cergy on the hill slopes overlooking and surrounding a meander in the river Oise. It is located around 32 kilometres/20 miles north-west of Paris and is easily accessible from there by fast suburban train or bus. The roughly rectangular 240-hectare/600-acre site was an old alluvial plain with a high water-table and wetland vegetation. Since the war extensive sand-quarrying had turned the area into a blighted collection of spoil-heaps and ponds, with a dense vegetation of willow, ash and alder overgrowing the banks between, with some poplar, oak and dying elm.

API's broad brief was to turn the site into a recreational landscape orientated to water-sports, with a catchment area of the whole Paris region as well as the local new town. A major complication was that the chief source of revenue for the scheme was profitable sand extraction. It had to continue throughout most of the landscape programme, in phase with its physical development. Planning was itself to some extent dependent on the physical needs of extraction, particular problems being posed in opening new parts of the site which were in close proximity to extraction works. An important priority was maintaining existing wildlife and its habitats; a visual constraint was to enhance the east–west visual link across the north section of the site between the bell tower of the church at old Cergy and the nearby castle of Vauréal.

Following long discussions with local people, sand dealers and officials API rejected the solution of digging out all the sand and making a vast lake in favour of creating an irregular water perimeter with islands and promontories, inlets and bays, using the available spoil for extensive land-forming: knolls, hills, valleys, slopes and plains.

The basic development principles included the establishment of several woodland areas densely planted with seedlings which would grow over a long term; also planting saplings and shrub clusters in

(*Below*) The master plan of Cergy Ponds: the Oise meanders around from the bottom right to the top right, its inner banks enclosing a series of lakes. The activity centres are on the right. The diagonal line across the left indicates the line of sight between the bell-tower of the church at Old Cergy and the château of Vauréal.

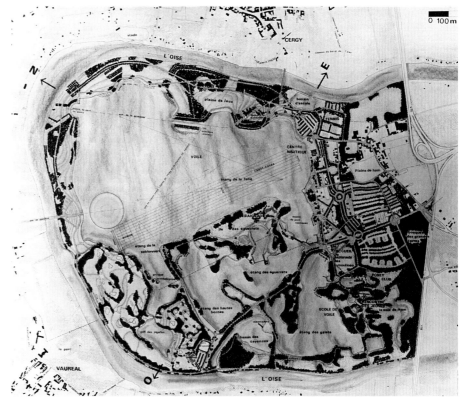

200

(**Above**) Aerial view of the landscape with the children's play and swimming area approached by a wooden bridge (*centre right*). The Oise circles around in the background.

(**Right**) One of the sylvan settings.

widely used areas and young trees in avenues and very heavily used areas. Marshlands were to be created on selected banks as habitats for aquatic animal life which could only be visited by supervised tours. Wild prairies were to be established for use only during the summer and spring. The basic planting was maple, larch, poplar, Corsican pine, oak and willow. The three primary criteria for selection of other planting were their foliage colour, their resistance to occasional flooding and their ability to attract wildlife and birds with fruit and berries.

The basic configuration of the new scheme is a series of irregular stretches of water between sometimes wooded and sometimes grassed promontories. In fact many of the lakes are interconnected with the main large lake, broken up visually by its boundary of woodland and prairie which itself borders the river Oise (except on the south side). It is a design theme repeated in the central island, which contains a swimming lake and a children's pool, originally designed with plastic Dayglo-coated concrete mounds and still retaining its playful water-pipes embedded in the slopes, with the addition of a ship half-buried in the sand. On other swimming beaches there are solaria and a wide variety of built facilities.

The main stretches of the lake are for sailing and canoeing, with a sailing school in an enclosed stretch of water to the south-west. There is an island designed to attract local and migrant wildfowl, and other sections of this enormous site are allocated to nature studies.

The stretch of land across the south of the site is intended for a variety of activities: riding, tennis, water games, a children's clubhouse; there is also the main reception entrance, which leads across a long wooden bridge to the swimming pond and children's playground on the central island. To the west is a farm and scattered around the perimeter of the lake are large grassed areas for play, forest walks among the dense vegetation, lookout points and, planned as the last stage when the final sand has been extracted, a nine-hole golf-course.

Although there is intense sporting activity the site is of such enormous size that it has been possible to design it as a vast naturalistic landscape, with heavy tree planting and fine detailing of the architectural elements, including such unexpected pleasures as giant insect sculptures located in hidden forest glades. With a site of this size and with its method of financing it is not surprising that work has been going on since as long ago as 1974, under a continual programme of maintenance by the local authority and development by the landscape designers.

(*Above*) **A giant insect, which visitors discover in a clearing.**

(*Opposite*) **A massive, simple timber bridge, its bolt-heads plainly visible, leads visitors to the lake within a lake forming the earliest development of the scheme.**

(*Left*) **Giant coloured nozzles emerge from the curving banks, spraying water over the play space (*left*).**

6.2
Richard Haag Associates

GAS WORKS PARK
Seattle, Washington
1973 to date
for Seattle City Council

In 1970 Richard Haag was commissioned to devise a master plan for a former gas plant on a promontory jutting 120 metres/400 ft out on the north side of Lake Union. Derelict and massively polluted, the windy 8-hectare/20.5-acre site was a major eyesore, visible from many parts of the city and most of the busy lake-shore.

The expected solution was a variation on the traditional civic arboretum landscape following massive detoxification of the ground. But that would have been very expensive. Haag anyway had developed a completely different approach. He had decided to work with what was already there, incorporating some of the old hated industrial plant and going with the history of the site rather than erasing it completely from memory. His proposals at first created an uproar in Seattle and the family of the woman after whom it was to be named refused permission. But following extensive public relations and consultation exercises, which Haag himself masterminded, the city decided to go ahead with the scheme, phased over a number of years.

The first stage involved trucking out the worst of the surface material, pipes and gas-making plant, and importing uncontaminated earth from a nearby construction site. It was thought that the deeper contamination of benzine and xylene could only be steamed out of the ground at great expense. But Haag took advice and argued that the better solution was to take advantage of the minerals and bacteria present in the subsoil and to introduce oil-eating enzymes and other organic matter in a series of deep tillings. These were carried out progressively with the addition of sewage sludge, grass clippings and compostable waste material. Their most important effect was to encourage soil and other bacteria to eat pollutants. This has remained a controversial solution and only time can tell how completely successful it is as a soil regeneration technique.

Haag developed a land-form strategy which left the cracking-towers on a ridge sloping down to the

(*Above*) The promontory of Gas Works Park from the east. The main mound rises above the docking area, with the range of old equipment in the background leading (*left*) to the big sheds enclosing brightly painted industrial engines from the original site.

(*Opposite*) Industrial archaeology: selected remnants of the old, hated gasworks plant form a major focus for Haag's new landscape.

(*Right*) Plan of the park: the main access road and parking are in the curve at the top; the mound is centre left, the range of retorts and crackers in the centre and the broad slope to the sound is at the right.

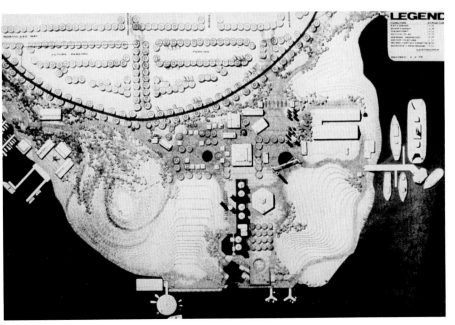

sea. To the north-east is a group of new barn-style buildings housing old machinery. Beyond that are picnic areas looking east over the lake. To the west Haag constructed a 15-metre/50-ft-high mound which has turned out to be the primary magnet for locals, who are not intent on playing among the brightly painted machinery to the east.

The rough grassed site is criss-crossed by paths and a lakeside promenade provides a prospect of the lake and access to landing jetties. The great mound is topped by a big sundial marked out with found materials. People tell the time by themselves acting as the gnomon and reading the position of their own shadow. The mound and its lakeward slopes are heavily used during the summer and its windy summit is a popular kite-flying venue.

Public authorities are preoccupied with safety, and some of the cracking-towers were fenced off from the public when two children injured themselves climbing among them. But Haag has been involved in a process of selective pruning of easily climbed elements of the towers and there has been a sugges-

tion that a moat might lessen the risk of public liability. His plans for the towers have included a vertical museum and a giant camera obscura.

The main visual feature of Gas Works Park is the range of cracking-towers, dark, rusting reminders of an industrial past only recently gone. In the playbarn nearby is a range of brightly coloured red, orange, yellow, blue and purple compressors and steam turbines and elsewhere there are visible reminders of the processes of the old gasworks serving as both found sculpture and as industrial archaeological ruins. All these retained elements are found objects which, rather than being fabricated together, have been the result of selective pruning – three-dimensional design by reduction rather than by assemblage. In the same 'found' spirit Haag has rejected the city's standard solution of year-round irrigation. He feels that it is proper that the rough grass, which is the main green element in the design, should follow its customary natural cycle of going brown in the summer, returning to green in the winter. Gas Works Park is not a landscape frozen for the foreseeable

(*Left*) Treeless, the landscape is a major attraction in warm weather for local people, who can sit, talk and watch the boats in the sound and kites being flown from the mound.

(*Above*) View from the big play sheds. The absence of planting and the rough grass are partly because of the poisons still being biodegraded in the earth beneath. They also reflect Haag's view that grass should flourish, turn brown in the hot summer and become dormant during the winter, rather than being neatly cut in municipal park fashion.

future in a formal mould. Its function is to provide the framework for an infinity of future possibilities, and above all to be used by people in ways of their own devising.

Haag's essential approach has been described by J. William Thompson as 'seeking out and preserving the spirit of place, doing more with less, deliberately simplifying one's means'. That is particularly apposite of Gas Works Park, whose very low budget and long time-scale has meant that Haag has not only had to develop a vision but remain responsive to possibilities which arise over the evolving life of his landscape – and remain politically adept and alert to the public bureaucracy which owns it.

6.3
Preben Jakobsen
BROADWATER PARK
Denham, Buckinghamshire, UK
1985
for the National Water Council

The UK National Water Council commissioned the Danish-born British landscape architect Preben Jakobsen to design the landscaping for a 5-hectare/12-acre office and industrial development on the site of the old Alexander Korda film studios on the river Colne in Buckinghamshire. The west boundary of the site is a busy highway, the east a wooded riverbank; to the south, over a busy minor road, are houses.

There was need for acoustic and visual shielding from the noisy roads, so Jakobsen deliberately defined the perimeter of the site with substantial earth-mounding, planting and, along one road, a sound-baffle wall.

The steeply sloping eastern riverside frontage had not been maintained for many years, and a number of dead and dangerous trees had to be removed. An early tree-surgery contract established which plant material could be retained; this included a number of yew and laurel hedges, which Jakobsen supple-

mented with additional planting in the same materials. Britain sometimes applies strict rules about nature conservation and a stringent land-management agreement had to be signed between the client and the local authority over the ecology of the river-bank. It is particularly sensitive because it faces across the river to an officially designated site of special scientific interest.

Much of the site is taken up with large industrial buildings, but the north quarter contains the more detailed part of Jakobsen's design around a mirror-glass office building, set back from the road on a raised podium planted with green laurels and large-leaved vitus. Jakobsen inserted a car park between the office building and the road and a smaller car park at right angles to the south-east of the building. Car-parking areas are one of the landscape designer's greatest problems. Dissatisfied with the standard solutions, he designed both of these as very formal areas; their plan is very similar to a hippodrome, with islands along the middle planted with multi-stemmed *Cercydiphyllum japonica*, birch and shrubs, including *Photinia*, laurel and viburnum. Both car parks are surrounded with ornamental plane trees and bamboo hedges, designed to emphasize the geometric formality of the layouts, with the entrances and exits defined by groups of trees and granite boulders.

The north-east corner of the site is overlooked by the long side of the office building and slopes increasingly steeply to the river, around 6 metres/20 ft lower in level. Here Jakobsen has created a formal area, bounded on the south side by plane trees and on the north by an herbaceous border with a background of trees and shrubs. Its main feature is a great

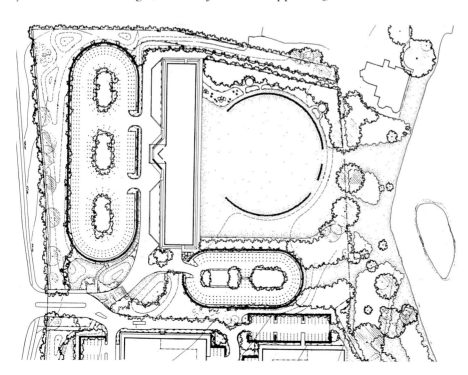

(*Left*) **Plan: the entrance is on the west (*bottom left*) with the smaller 'hippodrome' car park straight ahead. The main car park is to the north in front of the office building. The great circle to the east overlooks the steep slope down to the river on the right. To its north are the walks and sitting areas for staff.**

(*Right*) **Reflected in the glass walls of the office building, the extent of the herbaceous planting becomes slightly unclear.**

circular clipped hedge of field maple, which in section is a double square, 120 cm/4 ft wide and 240 cm/8 ft high. Slightly dished, the circle forms a shallow grass bowl. The hedge has a large gap near the office and two small gaps opposite to provide controlled views down to the river-valley and across to the vegetation on the opposite river-bank.

Between the curving hedge forming this enigmatic circle and the north boundary is a curvilinear garden for staff to sit out in the summer and hold meetings. It is defined on the north by an herbaceous border, with permanent shrubs among the herbaceous plants; the undulating boundary border is composed of trees and shrubs in silver-greys, blues and yellows. Distinctive vertical silvery grasses are contrasted with dome-shaped blue-grey shrubs. Grey-blue eucalyptus and yellow-green frisias surround seating areas; they contrast with the dark green of mature conifers in the background. This part of the landscape runs hard up against the mirrored face of the building, creating a nicely judged ambiguity with the landscape apparently continuing on through the glazed wall.

The visual theme of this northern area is of a dry watercourse leading down to the river, with smooth waterworn blue-grey flint pebbles, granite boulder groups and large circular exposed aggregate stepping-stones and sitting-platforms partially enclosed by sculptural steel palisades. The smaller circles deliberately echo the form of the great circle adjacent. The colours of the plants here change with the seasons – from blues and yellows in the summer to bronze and purples in the winter. The mix of shrubs and herbaceous material combined with large expanses of inert pebble ground-cover reduces the traditionally high cost of maintaining herbaceous borders.

Jakobsen's design belongs partly to one British tradition of highly detailed informal colour-planting and selection, and partly to a Danish tradition of

preoccupation with geometric formalism. In addition, the staff garden to the north of the great circle has certain resonances with the secret valley at Stowe, which is cut off from the great sloping lawn leading down to a lake. Inevitably the herbaceous border at Denham and Jakobsen's preoccupation with detailed planting elsewhere is reminiscent of the English tradition of Jekyll and Lutyens and is also a consequence of his own preliminary training as a horticulturalist at the Royal Botanic Gardens, Kew. Yet for the knowing it is slightly tongue-in-cheek – contemporary landscape designers deliberately avoid having much to do with flowering plants,

(*Top left*) The theme of this section of landscape to the north of the great circle is of a dried river-bed, with carefully placed granite rocks and blue-grey flint surrounded by planting which changes its colours according to the season.

which are thought to be the province of the lesser craft of ornamental gardening.

In contrast is the underlying formality of the scheme and the geometry of the great circle. It has clearly underlying symbolic intentions – perhaps the recycling of water, with which the client is involved. But it hints at more hermetic intentions, powerful forces; it is redolent of prehistoric settlements and monuments in England and Europe. And the circle is set in an essentially square framework – the squaring of the circle. The final broad intention is to create a heightened tension by deliberately seeking to juxtapose natural forms with stylized geometric forms.

(*Above*) The great circle surrounded by its growing hedge makes an enigmatic form, somewhat prehistoric in spirit, overlooking the river Colne and the protected site of special scientific interest on the opposite bank.

6.4
Daniel D. Stewart
TOAD HALL
East Hampton, New York
1983
for a private client

Daniel Stewart's client wanted to make a serious statement about design at her 8-hectare/20-acre Atlantic Ocean estate on Long Island. Part of a design team which included the architects Gwathmey Siegel, Stewart was responsible for all the exterior work on the virgin site, a long narrow plot of land which stretches north from the seashore back through the tertiary dunes to the access road. Local nature conservancy groups insisted that the three or four hectares/ eight or ten acres of primary and secondary dunes remain in their natural state. The 5 hectares/12 acres of tertiary dunes, with their woods, secondary growth and brambles, form the setting for the residence, which includes the main house with a swimming-pool to one side and a series of semi-formal spaces progressing back towards the access road. In order, these are a croquet lawn, a cutting garden with guest-house and garage to the west and a sunken tennis court. Beyond there is an area of naturalized planting and finally a small lake and an entrance. Beyond this the access path from the house takes a dog-leg to the east and out to the main road. It is a development of sequential landscape spaces which starts at the greenhouse built into the corner of

(*Below*) **Plan: the entrance is from the north, with its dog-leg around the north of the lake and then in a long stretch to the house. The secondary and primary dunes and the ocean are to the right. The tennis-court, cutting garden and croquet lawn are to the east, above the guesthouse and garages.**

(*Right*) **The lake, surrounded by local and naturalized planting.**

(*Opposite below*) **The formal entrance, actually well inside the site, is through a broken stuccoed wall in pink, a homage to the Mexican designer Luis Barragán; a satellite dish is mounted in the water.**

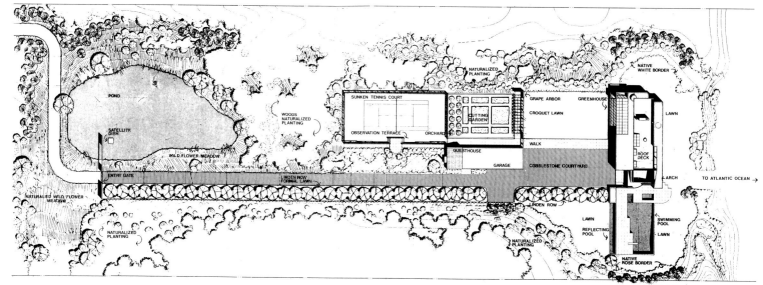

the house, serving as an interface between inside and outside.

On the other hand the sequence can be read in the opposite direction. From the main road the entrance road takes a right bend, revealing the small lake surrounded by naturalized wild flowers and trees. A second bend reveals the entrance, a free-standing pink stucco wall reminiscent of the work of Luis Barragán. The wall is broken cleanly on either side of the road, framing the long vista down to the house and its attenuated square 'arch' framing the dunes and the Atlantic beyond. The east section of wall stretches into the lake, with a large rectangular opening forming a 'bridge' over the lake edge. A satellite dish is mounted on a plinth in the water in front of the far section of wall. Here are the main

visual elements which are to continue through the landscape: high technology, soft-edged nature and soft, friendly architecture. At the gap in the entrance wall the road surface changes abruptly from gravel to granite. It is laid in courses across the road, with longitudinal granite edges. On the right is a narrow lawn planted with formally spaced linden trees backed by naturalized and local planting. On the left are wild flowers and trees around the lake and woodland and increasingly clear glimpses of the designed elements of the landscape and architecture.

At the house the paving widens to form a court-yard and the turf under the lindens on the other side spreads out to the west to form a roughly triangular lawn, the south side of which is defined by a pink stucco wall behind a linear reflecting pool. On the other side of the wall is the swimming-pool and deck. The lawn, bordered with native rose plants, encircles the end of the wall and runs around the raised swimming-pool, across the front of the house and its terrace and round the other side to the end of the greenhouse, where it forms another semicircular area edged with white native plants. This White Garden is overlooked from the living-room. The lawn serves the traditional front living-area function of front lawns – and also as the transition between house and dunes and ocean.

On the other side of the house a secondary green slate walkway links the main entrance with the distant tennis court. The manicured croquet lawn immediately in front is separated from the cutting garden behind it by a grape arbour with pink stucco 'bastions' at each end. The cutting garden is sur-

(*Above*) The forecourt to the house, designed by Gwathmey Siegel in greying timber siding with its integral conservatory (*left*) overlooking the croquet lawn. The swimming pool is off to the right.

(*Left*) Carefully laid granite paving leads south to the house, with a formal row of lindens to the right and the naturalized planting of the area to the left, behind which is the lake.

rounded by a rose-covered fence and the court by trees.

All the planting is either native to Long Island or planting which has been naturalized to the local environment. Unlike many landscape architects, Stewart has been unafraid of introducing flowers: in spring there are soft blooms all over the site and in the warm summer months massed colours are grouped around the lake, single colours in the rose and white gardens on either side of the house.

Toad Hall represents a subtle interplay between the wild natural environment and the geometry of designed elements. The latter are organized on a grid whose underlying consistency ties them together with an invisible but clarifying order. The croquet lawn, cutting garden and tennis court are in a sense extensions of the architecture, as is the axial granite access road. The tennis court is sunk in order to soften its impact on the wild landscape beyond. The drama and ultimately vast scale of the ocean environment called for an ordering, contrasting geometry, for people were to live here. So there is a continual play between formal and informal, natural and man-made, soft and sharp edges, wild and manicured, a theme of balance between nature in the raw and the intelligent works of man.

(*Top*) **The swimming pool with its sheltering wall and, beyond, the rose garden.**

(*Right*) **The grape arbour of the cutting garden, the central of the three formal spaces on axis with the conservatory. Pink stuccoed bastions indicate the formal division between this garden and the croquet lawn behind.**

6.5
The Office of Peter Walker
SOLANA
Westlake/Southlake, Texas
1990

for IBM, Maguire Thomas Partners

Peter Walker was responsible for the site analysis and planning, the criteria for physical development, the open-space master-plan and the overall landscape design for Solana, a 350-hectare/850-acre office park 12 kilometres/8 miles north-west of the Dallas–Fort Worth airport, being developed by an IBM–Maguire Thomas Partnership joint venture.

The site lies laterally across a highway running diagonally from north-west to south-east. The site and its surrounding prairies and woodlands are rolling grazed pastureland and uplands which contain some of the last stands of post oak in the area. The eastern section, Southlake, was primarily wooded, the western section more prairie-like, with a ridge circling round the south-west.

Walker's brief was to enhance the whole site by treating it as one grand landscape to provide a context for the buildings, to create a contemporary identity for the scheme with massing of forms and amenities at a human scale.

He argued for a remarkably low building-to-landscape ratio, which preserved the uplands curving around the south-west of the site, a large area of pasture and a meadow between the office buildings and the highway. The area has hot dry summers and cold, often harshly windy winters. Water and natural vegetation are precious, so that natural creek beds, trees and the pattern of existing vegetation determined the location of building plots set within

(*Below*) Contrasts of rigid geometry generated by the form of the buildings cutting across the designed naturalistic waterway in front of the main compounds.

(*Opposite*) Water and building and geometric ground patterns combined with formal planting integrate with each other and with the main visual structure of the layout.

landscape 'rooms'. Building height was restricted to five storeys, so that from the highway the architecture would always be backed by the wooded ridge and its associated hills and given a foreground of meadows and their richly colourful native planting. Parking, a major landscape problem in all office developments, is located primarily in formal covered parking buildings, only a quarter of them visible, in very heavily tree-shaded 'orchards'.

Walker has been at pains to maintain the existing cover and vegetation, to pave as little as possible and to maintain the continuity of existing drainage. Pastureland is refurbished by using native seeds, which require no watering and will grow to a height of six feet with several annual flowerings.

The entrance off the highway to both sides of the site is delineated by rectangles of planting which are intended to suggest a somewhat agricultural air. They have highly stylized diagonal rows of Indian hawthorn, planted rather like vineyards. Some of these blocks are level, others tilted. In one section a pool is fed by runnels spilling through square holes in an enclosing wall.

The IBM marketing and technical support centre at the entrance to the north-east Southlake section of the site was designed by Legorreta Arquitectos in a somewhat hacienda style: it has strongly coloured stucco walls and rambling building forms with sloping diagonal walls extending out far beyond the perimeter of the buildings. In some cases they interact with canals and formal patterns of planting.

On the south side of the highway entrance is the village centre. The centrepiece for its hotel approach is a Walker-designed domed mist fountain in concentric layers of precisely carved Arizona flagstones 15 metres/49 ft in diameter and more than 2 metres/6 ft high, backed by double rows of potted Italian cypress. The dome has five vertical slices and one not quite horizontal. Puffs of mist spray from the geometric fissures in a way which calls to mind the prehistoric or the geological. Coloured light from the main cross-fissure changes from gold to violet on a repeating 90-minute timescale.

The office sector in the north-west section of the site is made up of four compounds radiating out from the meadow south of the highway. Between the two is a great semi-formal grassed space 9,000 metres/3,000 ft long, in three terraces. It is here that the geometry of the buildings is reflected in the

(*Top*) An aerial view of the central section either side of the highway, with intimations of agricultural patterning in the foreground.

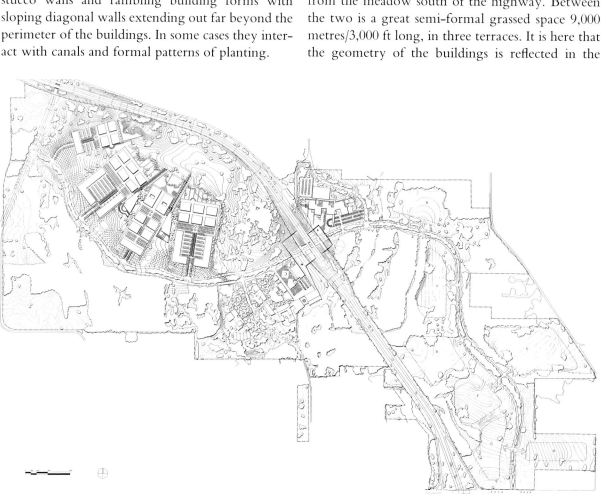

(*Opposite below*) Plan: the entrance complex either side of the highway (*centre*); the eastern development with the four main compounds centred on the meadow (*top left*). Reinforced existing planting is to the west and south. On the right are plots for subsequent development in woodland glades.

(*Above*) Overlayering of geometries: channels slice through the opposing direction of the low wall and, enigmatically, stop.

adjacent landscape. There are long straight paths, canals and rows of trees skewing across the great terrace; along its northern edge meanders a wooded canal threading through a range of outdoor rooms: a naturalistic grove, a dining grove, circular curving and straight hedges and radial canals. The meander is in effect the boundary between the hard-edged built sections and the soft natural areas.

(*Opposite*) The courtyard in the central public zone of Solana.

(*Right*) The domed sculpture from whose fissures rise puffs of mist and a slowly changing cycle of lights.

(*Below*) Reminiscent of a formal parterre, this set-piece also has resonances of local agricultural planting patterns.

The parkway round the south of the building compounds in this western section serves the same function in a rather more conventional way: its curving path, following the line of the ridge behind, separates natural woodland from the severe geometry of the buildings and their formal approach roads, with the painted stucco parking buildings forming a background to the heavy formal planting of the parks.

At the entrance to the first IBM compound are two stone rings, one black and one white, with a line of mist wisp aligned on the centre of the tree-lined entrance road. Elsewhere a mysterious circular fountain is enclosed in a pine grove: a pale blue ring, it encloses a sunken garden of stone and ground-cover plants, with a fine mist rising from the middle, providing a micro-climate for the exotic plants.

Solana has had extensive earth-mounding works. They are analogous to the extensive remodelling of, say, Brown, Repton or Olmsted, where nature is subtly accommodated rather than defied. Walker's aim has been to preserve as much of the feeling of the existing surrounding landscape as possible, and, where buildings occur, to effect a transition which has the quality of agricultural settlements: the deployment of expected and unexpected geometries and repetitions; of the creative use of water, primordial and mysterious in special places, canal-like and arbitrary in others, casual and gentle on the rim of the grassed prairie.

(*Above*) **The entrance to the IBM compound: inscrutable stone rings with wisps of mist hint at prehistoric rituals.**

(*Right*) **Carefully cut stepping-stones across the formal canal.**

6.6
Roger DeWeese Inc. & Associates

WATERIDGE CORPORATE BUSINESS PARK

San Diego, California
1983
for Equidon Investment Builders

Roger DeWeese had been part of the master-planning team for a barren 50-hectare/125-acre site east of Interstate 805 above the Sorrento Valley, San Diego. The county had designated it as suitable for research and development firms. Several clients had come and gone and land values had risen as each planning application had revealed more of the site's potential. Equidon Investment Builders took on the site and gave the team a brief to develop it as a very high-quality business park whose environment would lure high-technology industries from places such as Silicon Valley in northern California. Equidon knew that staff costs for this kind of industry were ten times their office-space costs and that superb

working environments were a major factor in firms keeping and attracting high-quality staff.

Unusually for landscape projects, which are frequently merely a cosmetic addition at the end of a building programme, this was a scheme which was driven by the landscape programme, not least because until the first commercial offices were built the landscape was all there was to set the mood and image for early prospective property purchasers.

DeWeese was faced with the technical problems of a treeless, rather lumpy site with soil which could support only local scrub and grasses. His planning problem was to programme landscape development on a site which would eventually be 30 per cent taken up by 25 buildings, but at an uncertain rate of building development dependent on the state of the market. His visual problem was how to create an entirely new environment visible from relatively distant views including the freeway, which at the same time both worked on an intimate pedestrian scale within the site, and made sense in the periods between building programmes.

The creation of an entirely artificial landscape meant importing many tens of thousands of cubic yards of good quality topsoil which was used gradually, as landscape construction, land-forming and planting took place. It also meant selecting a range of planting which could cope with the modified

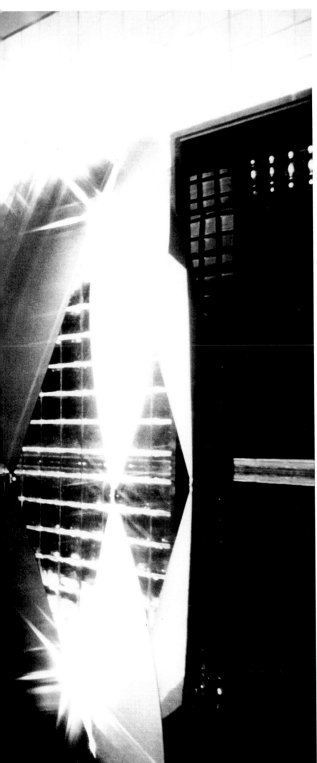

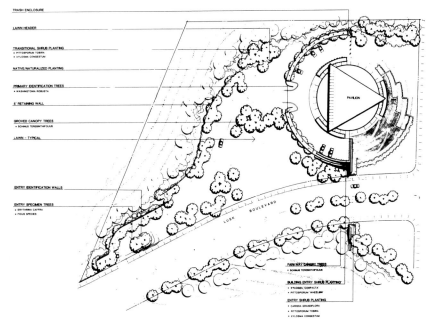

(*Left*) **The selling pavilion rising out of the circular reflecting pool, with young trees and very carefully selected planting. Before this was constructed the site was barren scrubland dotted with large ungainly hillocks. The water in this pool serves as a holding tank for the waterfalls and cascades. Thousands of gallons of water are recycled each minute.**

(*Above*) **Plan of the selling pavilion and its earth-formed surroundings: a winding path leads up to the circular platform and the triangular building apparently sitting across a circular pool, with the cascade to the right.**

environment, including tall palms, which have been used to define axes, avenues and formal areas. It meant, too, devising and installing a comprehensive irrigation system for grass and other planting. The system selected uses solar-powered irrigation controllers and moisture-sensing devices on all the slope irrigation systems. Water was not simply needed for irrigation: it forms a major element in the master-plan, which incorporates aqueducts, canals, water-falls, lakes and pools using mainly recycled water.

The first formal composition on site was the sales office, an 800-square-metre/8,800-square-ft triangular pavilion faced with foot-square glass bricks and set over a circular pool at the top of a semicircular promontory. A formal exercise in monumental geometry, the building has access at grade level; the other half of the circular plan is formed by a great stepped truncated half-cone, down which cascade thousands of gallons of water. The ensemble of the rippling curved staircase of water and the glass wall of the pavilion reflecting the moving water in the semicircular pool above creates an eye-catching and somewhat ambiguous effect of movement. A retaining wall between the high-level car park and the stepped cascade has an adjacent pool whose water drops 8 metres/25 ft into the low-level perimeter canal and is mirrored by a similar cascade on the other side of the public boulevard – the two were originally intended to be joined by an aqueduct.

(**Right**) **The first landscape work at Wateridge, the selling pavilion, an integration of architecture and landscape. The great curving cascade of water ripples down a truncated cone with Renaissance-inspired stairs leading up through the water. Above it, the foot-square glass blocks of the triangular building have** the same shimmering quality as the water.

(**Top**) **The wall in the centre carries a narrow channel of water along its top which falls dramatically to the collecting channel below. Across the road a similar wall serves as the other side of a 'gateway' to the development.**

One of the delights of the main cascade is the pair of staircases, 45 stairs in a double chevron formation, which march up the cascade in a manner reminiscent of grassed stairways in formal Renaissance gardens. The fact that there is no pedestrian access to the stairway except from above is in a sense irrelevant: visitors come to the building by car. According to the financial logic of the area, the cascade is actually much more economical of scarce water than if grass had been planted and permanently irrigated.

De Weese has continued the water theme in the first commercial development on the site: three low-rise office buildings in a triangular formation around a tight plaza. Alongside the main entrance a thin sheet of water hugs a vertical burgundy-coloured slate wall and, after following the side of a stair into the plaza, cascades over large blocks of square-cut slate arranged in a rough chevron configuration, down to an irregular pool and thence via canals to the other exits between the buildings.

The pavilion design deploys water as a three-dimensional element – designed to be seen, to attract attention, to serve as a deliberately ambiguous solid whose ambiguities are to do with formal shapes and with the reflecting qualities of the pavilion and its unseen (from road level at least) reflecting pool. Among the offices it serves a more conventional function, introducing an irregular quasi-natural contrast to the regular forms of the surrounding buildings; it also has the functional virtue of mitigating a 10 metre/30-ft climb between the buildings and their car parks underneath.

(*Above*) The water feature in the first commercial office development provides sympathetic contrast with the rectangular buildings by using stonework of similar colours and by reintroducing irregular visual elements. The run-off water threads its way through a central triangular courtyard between the three buildings.

(*Right*) The landscape architects have deliberately used the experience of water rushing, and in other places moving placidly, to mitigate the experience of climbing as many as 30 stairs to the ground floors of the office buildings.

PROJECT TEAMS

1.1 WILSHIRE PLAZA POCKET PARK, Los Angeles
Fong, Preston, Jung Associates (Fong and Associates, Inc.), 930 W. 16th Street, Suite A2, Costa Mesa, CA 92627
(714) 645 9444
Designer: Allen Don Fong
Contractor: C.L. Peck

1.2 SEATTLE FREEWAY PARK, Seattle, Washington
Lawrence Halprin, 444 Brannan Street, San Francisco, CA 94107
(415) 546 1952
Design team: Lawrence Halprin and Associates

1.3 PIAZZA D'ITALIA, New Orleans, Louisiana
Charles Moore, 1063 Gayley, Los Angeles, CA 90024
Designer: Charles Moore
Associated architects: Allen Eskew and Malcolm Heard Jr of Perez Associates and Ron Filson

1.4 HARLEQUIN PLAZA, Greenwood Village, Colorado
SWA Group, 2200 Ridgeway Boulevard, Sausalito, CA 94964
(415) 332 5100
Design team: George Hargreaves, William Callaway, Danny Powell, Tom Adams, Mike Sardina
Associated architects: Gensler & Associates

1.5 JARDINS DE TURIA, Valencia
Ricardo Bofill, Taller de Arquitectura, Av. Industria, 14 - 08960 Sant Just Desvern, Barcelona, Spain
(93) 371 59 50
Project director: P. Dillon
Project team: F. Trueba, X. Grau, O.Migliore, J. Montlló
Production team: J.A. Coderch (director), R. Vivancos
Structural consultant: F. Rubio
Engineering consultant: V. Gonzales
Contractor: Cubiertas y Dalmau SA

1.6 LONGFELLOW GARDEN, New York
Weintraub & di Domenico, Suite 2D, 181 Hudson Street, New York, NY 10013
(212) 431 8514
Landscape architects: Lee Weintraub, John di Domenico
Project landscape architect: Jose Cheing
Team: Richard Sullivan and Steven Whitesel
In conjunction with the City of New York's Department of Housing Preservation and Development
Consultant architects: Pumilia, Falko & Wicher
Contractor: Doyle Baldante Construction Corporation

2.1 PARQUE TEZOZOMOC, Azcapotzalco, Mexico City
Grupo de Diseño Urbano SC, 06700 Orizaba, 125 Col. Roma, Mexico DF
(525) 553 1248
Design team: Mario Schjetnan, Jorge Calvillo, Jose Luis Perez, Manuel Peniche
Historical consultant: Thomas Cavillo
Graphic design: D.I. Jorge Sandoval

2.2 SAN JOSE PLAZA PARK, California
George Hargreaves, Hargreaves Associates, 855 Folsom Street, Suite 205, San Francisco, CA 94107
(415) 543 4957
Design team: George Hargreaves, Mary Margaret Jones, Peter Geraghty, Dennis Taniguchi, Glenn Allen
Consultants: Structural Design Engineers, Fountain Tech, MTH Engineers
Contractors: Collishaw Construction, Pacific Water Art, Torres Concrete

2.3 SUTTON PLACE, Surrey, UK
Designer: Sir Geoffrey Jellicoe

2.4 LE PARC DE LA CORDERIE ROYALE, Rochefort-sur-Mer, France
Bernard Lassus, 4 Rue Benard, 75014 Paris
(331) 45 43 47 82
Design team: Bernard Lassus, Pascal Aubry, Alain Mazas and Pierre Donadieu

2.5 CLAREMONT, Surrey, UK
National Trust supervising agent: Peter Masefield
Historical adviser: Christopher Berharral
National Trust gardens adviser: Graham Thomas
Head gardener: Arnold Amess

2.6 GRAND MALL PARK, Yokohama, Japan
Tokyo Landscape Architects, Inc., Meito Building, 1–16–4 Jingumae Shibuya-ku, Tokyo, Japan
Project manager: Haruto Kobayashi
Conceptual planner: Tatsushi Yamanaka
Construction planner: Tsuneo Suzuki
Associated designers: Mikiko Ishii Design, Office Lighting Design
Contractors: Sakaata, Fuji Construction, Mitsuhashi Ryokka

2.7 J. PAUL GETTY MUSEUM, Malibu, California
Emmet L. Wemple, 2503A West Seventh Street, Los
    Angeles, CA 90057
(213) 386 6623
Historical consultant: Norman Neuerburg
Landscape contractor: Moulder Brothers
Building contractor: Dinwiddie Construction Company

3.1 RIO SHOPPING CENTER, Atlanta, Georgia
The Office of Peter Walker/Martha Schwartz: principal,
    Martha Schwartz, 2140 Bush Street, #2, San
    Francisco, CA 94115
(415) 922 1330
Design team: Martha Schwartz, Ken Smith, Doug
    Findlay, David Meyer, David Walker, Martin Poirier
Associated architects: Arquitectonica, Coral Gables
Production architects: Milton Pate & Associates
Contractor: McDevitt & Street

3.2 PARQUE DEL CLOT, Barcelona
Dani Freixes with Vicente Miranda, C. Carmen 44/3.2,
    08001 Barcelona, Spain
(93) 301 4297
Design: Dani Freixes and Vicente Miranda
Design team: Eulalia Gonzalez, Victor Argentí, Chechu
    Sanz, Dolors Andreu, Manuel Ruisanchez
Surveyor: Felix Force
Structural consultants: Jesus Jimenez and Alfonso Garcia-
    Pozuelo, Luis Moya
Contractors: Cubiertas y Mzov

3.3 FOUNTAIN PLAZA, Dallas, Texas
Dan Kiley, Kiley/Walker, East Farm, Charlotte,
    Vermont 05445, USA
(802) 425 2141
Landscape architect: Daniel Urban Kiley
Partner in charge: Peter Ker Walker
Associated architects: Pei, Cobb, Freed & Partners
Structural engineers: CBM Engineers
Landscape contractors: Saias Gelrud, San Felipe
    Landscaping

3.4 PARC DE LA VILLETTE, Paris
Bernard Tschumi, NY: (212) 807 6340; NY, Columbia
    University, (212) 280 4444 and 3473; Paris: (331) 42 39
    21 48
Project team: Bernard Tschumi, Luca Merlini,
    Alexandra Villegas, Luca Pagnamenta
Landscape: William Wallis of Balsley Associates, Phoebe
    Cutler

3.5 BAMBOO GARDEN, Parc de la Villette, Paris
Alexandre Chemetoff, Bureau des Paysages, 119 Rue du
    Château, 75014 Paris
(331) 43 27 62 72
Design team: Alexandre Chemetoff, Martine Renan
Associated artists: Daniel Buren, Bernard Leitner
Architectural consultant: Jean-Louis Cohen
Engineering consultant: Henri Bardsley

4.1 STOCKLEY PARK, London
Master planners, architects, engineers and quantity
    surveyors: Arup Associates, 2 Dean St, London
    W1V 6QB
(071) 734 8494
Landscape architects: Ede Griffiths Partnership

4.2 NMB BANK, Amsterdam
J'ørn Copijn, Copijn Utrecht, Postbus 9177, 3506 GD,
    Utrecht, Gageldijk 4 F, and Peter Rawstorne
    Associates, Dunsdale, Forest Row, East Sussex
    RH18 5BD, UK
(0342) 82 2704
Landscape contractors: Copijn Utrecht Groenadviseurs
Sculptural details: Rawstorne
Architect: A. Alberts, Amsterdam
Construction engineering consultants: Raadgevend
    Ingenieursbureau Aronsohn BV, Rotterdam
Mechanical engineering consultants: Technisch
    Adviesbureau Treffers en Partners, Baarn

4.3 ROBSON SQUARE, Vancouver
Arthur Erickson Architects, Inc., 2412 Laurel Street,
    Vancouver, British Columbia, Canada V5Z 3T2
(604) 879 0211
Landscape architects: Cornelia Hahn Oberlandser, Ken
    Morris, Robert Zinzer, Raoul Robillard
Urban design: Dennis Christianson, Alan Bell
Structural engineering: Bogue Babicki & Associates

4.4 WINTER GARDEN, Niagara Falls, NY
M. Paul Friedberg & Partners, 41 East 11th Street, New
    York, NY 10003
(212) 477 6366
Design team: Mark Morrison, Seymour Katzman
Architect: Gruen Associates
Design architect: Cesar Pelli
Interior landscape contractor: The Everett Conklin
    Companies

4.5 CAPABILITY GREEN, Bedfordshire, UK
Robert Holden, Clifton Design, 8 Bristol Gardens,
    London W9 2JG
(071) 286 6622
Master-planners: Bruce Gilbreth Architects
Landscape architects: Brian Clouston & Partners,
    succeeded by Clifton Design
Special landscapes: Rosemary Verey

4.6 TSUKUBA CIVIC CENTRE, Tsukuba
    Academic New Town, Japan
Arata Isozaki Associates, 6-17 9-Chome, Minato-ku,
    Tokyo 107, Japan
(813) 405 1526 /475 5265
Design team: Shuichi Fujie, Takashi Ito, Hiroshi Aoki,
    Makoto Watanabe, Hideo Matsura
Sculptor: Hidetoshi Nagasawa
Structural consultants: Toshio Kimura Structural
    Engineers
Mechanical consultants: Kankyo Engineering Inc.

Landscape contractors: Keio Landscape Garden Planning Co.
Contractor: Toda Corporation/Tobishima Construction/Ohki Construction/Kabuki Construction joint endeavour

4.7 BRION FAMILY CEMETERY, S. Vito, Italy
Designer: Carlo Scarpa

5.1 SPINOZA'S GARDEN, Architecture Biennale, The Netherlands
Designer: Raoul Bunschoten
Team: Simon Miller, Toke Kharnpej, Greta Stokka, David Gregory, Michael Beacon, David Evans, Imanudin Ghazali, Jeffrey Molder, David Racz, Richard Smith, Edith Soleiman

5.2 EMILIO'S FOLLY
Emilio Ambasz, 632 Broadway, New York, NY 10012
(212) 420 8850
Designer: Emilio Ambasz
Illustrator: Dwight Ashdown
Model-maker: Toshio Okumura

5.3 LITTLE SPARTA, Dunsyre, Scotland, UK
Designer: Ian Hamilton Finlay, Stonypath, Little Sparta, Dunsyre, Lanark ML11 8GN
(089) 981 252

5.4 AICHI GREEN CENTRE, Japan
Robert K. Murase, Murase Associates, 1300 N.W. Northrup, Portland, OR 97209, USA
(503) 242 1477
Landscape architect: Robert Murase
Master-planner: Hajime Nakamura

5.5 FOUR CONTINENTS BRIDGE, Hiroshima, Japan
SITE Projects Ibc
Design team: Joshua Weinstein, James Wines, Glen Coben
Structural engineers: Geiger, Gossen & Hamilton
Landscape consultant: Signe Nielson
Lighting design: Quentin Thomas Associates
Contractor: Takenaka Komuten Co

5.6 CALIFORNIA SCENARIO, Costa Mesa, California
Designer: Isamu Noguchi
Contractor: C.J. Segerstrom and Sons
Landscape consultant: Kammeyer and Partners

5.7 EUDOXIA
Michael Van Valkenburgh, 1158 Massachusetts Avenue, Cambridge, MA 02139, USA
(617) 864 4233

5.8 CITY CENTRE PARK, Milton Keynes, Buckinghamshire, UK
Designer: Andrew Mahaddie, Milton Keynes Development Corporation Architects

5.9 TERRAIN, O' Hare International Center, Chicago
Elyn Zimmerman, c/o Siteline Fine Arts Corporation, 39 Worth Street, New York, NY 10013
Consultant architects: Holabird & Root
Landscape consultants: Iverson Perennial Gardens, Hayden Landscape Contractors, Bill Ruth, Freeman Hills Associates
Contractor: O'Neil Construction

6.1 BASE DE PLEIN AIR ET LOISIRS, Cergy Neuville, France
API – Etude de Paysage, 11 Rue Dieu, 75010 Paris
(331) 42 08 48 40
Design team: Paul Brichet, Andreas Jaeggli, Michel Viollet
Infrastructure consultants: SEBA and Ove Arup
Landscape contractors: Guintoli, Morillon-Corvol, Val d'Oise Paysage, Prettre, Savpo, Sevoise, CIDRD

6.2 GAS WORKS PARK, Seattle, Washington
Richard Haag Associates, Inc., 2923 Fuhman Ave East, Seattle, WA 98102
(206) 634 1020
Design team: Richard Haag Associates
Landscape contractors: Sun Up Landscape Construction, Davis Court Inc.

6.3 BROADWATER PARK, Denham, Buckinghamshire, UK
Preben Jakobsen, Jakobsen Landscape Architects, Mount Sorrel, West Approach Drive, Pittville, Cheltenham GL52 3AD
(0242) 241501
Contractor: Jakobsen and Frost Landscape Construction

6.4 TOAD HALL, East Hampton, NY
Stewart Associates, 237 West 18th Street, New York, NY 10001
(212) 989 0642
Landscape architect: Daniel D. Stewart
Associated architects: Gwathmey Siegel
Contractors: Caramanga & Murphy, Lewis & Valentine

6.5 SOLANA, Westlake/Southlake, Texas
The Office of Peter Walker and Partners, 2222 Bush Street, San Francisco, CA 94115
(415) 922 4535
Landscape architects: Peter Walker, Doug Findlay, Tony Sinkosky, Tom Leader, Lisa Roth, David Walker, Rob Rombold
Design architects: Mitchell/Giurgola Architects, Ricardo Legorretta Architectos
Engineers: Carter and Burgess, Inc.

Planning: Barton Myers Associates
Water features: Howard Fields and Associates, J. Harlan
  Glenn and Associates, Rock and Waterscapes, Inc.
Graphics and signage: SOM, San Francisco
General contractor: HCB Contractors

6.6 WATERIDGE CORPORATE BUSINESS PARK,
San Diego, California

Roger DeWeese Inc./DeWeese Burton Associates, 1302
  Carmino del Mar, Del Mar, CA 92014
(619) 453 7371
Designer: Roger DeWeese, Inc., & Associates
Architect: WZMH
Fountain consultant: CMS
Civil engineers: Sholders & Sandford
Landscape contractor: Valley Crest

BIBLIOGRAPHY

GENERAL

Books

Alphand, J.C.A., *Les Promenades de Paris*, Paris, 1867–73.
Ambasz, Emilio, *The Architecture of Luis Barragán*, New
  York, 1976.
Church, Thomas, *Gardens are for People*, New York,
  1955.
Crowe and Miller, *Shaping Tomorrow's Landscape*,
  Amsterdam, 1964.
Downing, A.J., *A Treatise on the Theory and Practice of
  Landscape Gardening Adapted to North America*, New
  York, 1841.
Eckbo, Garrett, *Landscape for Living*, New York, 1950.
Fein, A., *Frederick Law Olmsted and the American
  Environmental Tradition*, New York, 1972.
Hunt, John Dixon and Willis, Peter, *The Genius of the
  Place*, New York, 1975.
Hussey, Christopher, *The Picturesque*, London, 1927.
Jekyll, Gertrude, *Colour in the Flower Garden*, London,
  1908.
Jellicoe, Geoffrey and Susan, *The Landscape of Man*,
  London, 1975.
McHarg, Ian, *Design with Nature*, New York, 1969.
Manwaring, Elizabeth Wheeler, *Italian Landscape in
  Eighteenth-Century England*, London, 1965.
Masson, Georgina, *Italian Gardens*, London, 1961.
Moore, Mitchell, Turnbull, *The Poetics of Gardens*,
  Cambridge, 1989.

Noguchi, Isamu, *A Sculptor's World*, London, 1967.
Papadakis, Cooke, Benjamin, *Deconstruction*, London,
  1989.
Robinson, William, *The Wild Garden*, London, 1870.
Stroud, Dorothy, *Capability Brown*, London, 1975.
Stroud, Dorothy, *Humphry Repton*, London, 1962.
Tunnard, Christopher, *Gardens in the Modern Landscape*,
  London, 1938.
various, *Elyn Zimmerman, a Decade of Projects*, New
  York, 1988.
various, *Emilio Ambasz, the Poetics of the Pragmatic*, New
  York, 1988.
Watkin, David, *The English Vision*, London, 1982.
Weibenson, Dora, *The Picturesque Garden in France*,
  Princeton, 1978.
Willis, Peter, *Charles Bridgeman and the English Landscape
  Garden*, London, 1977.
Woodbridge, Kenneth, *Landscape and Antiquity: aspects of
  English culture at Stourhead 1718–1838*, Oxford, 1970.

Periodical articles

Allen, Gerald, 'The Lay of the Land', *Places*, vol. 4, n. 4.
Anderton, Frances, 'Avant-gardens', *Architectural
  Review*, September 1989, pp. 32–41.
Architecture d'Aujourd'hui, December 1981.
Architectural Record, vol. 116, October 1954, pp. 145–151
  & p. 324.
Bann, Stephen, 'From Captain Cook to Neil
  Armstrong: colonial exploration and the structure of
  landscape', in *Projecting the landscape*, Humanities
  Research Centre, Australian National University,
  1987, pp. 79–91.
Bann, Stephen and Lassus, Bernard, 'The Landscape
  Approach of Bernard Lassus', *Journal of Garden
  History*, April/June 1983, pp. 79–107.
Boyle Family, *Landscape Architecture* (UK), August 1987,
  pp. 36–7.
Buchanan, Peter, *Architectural Review*, 1988, Vol. 2, pp.
  72–3.
Buchanan, Peter, 'Ambasz urban gardens', *Architectural
  Review*, September 1989, pp. 49–59.
Chang Chin-Yu (ed), 'Works by Lawrence Halprin',
  Process Architecture, No. 4, November 1981.
'Dan Kiley', *Process Architecture*, October 1982, whole
  issue.

_____*Landscape Architecture*, January/February 1988, p.60.

_____*Landscape Architecture*, July/August 1986, pp. 48ff.

_____*Landscape Design*, August 1979.

Davey, Peter, 'The rebirth of the garden', *Architectural Review*, September 1989, p. 31.

Dwyer, Garry, 'The Power under our Feet', *Landscape Architecture*, May/June 1986, pp. 65–68.

'Earthworks past and present', *Art Journal*, #42. Fall 1982, pp. 191, 233–267.

'Ernst Cramer', *Anthos* 2/1987, pp. 1–37.

'Ernst Cramer 1898–1980', *Anthos*, 2/1987, pp. 1–37.

Frey, Susan Rademacher, 'Hargreaves Associates', *Progressive Architecture*, July 1989.

'Garrett Eckbo', *Architectural Record*, vol. 87, pp. 73–79; vol. 86, pp. 68–74; vol. 85, pp. 70–71.

_____*Progressive Architecture*, September 1986, 5&9, pp. 23–25

_____*Landscape Architecture*, November/December 1986, pp. 78–79.

Halprin, Lawrence, *Progressive Architecture*, September 1986, 5&9, pp. 23–25.

Hargreaves, George, 'Point of View', *Landscape Architecture*, November/December 1986, pp. 52–53, 110, 112.

_____'Post-Modernism looks beyond itself', *Landscape Architecture*, July 1983, pp. 60–65.

Ikehara, Kenichiro, 'Japanese Memorial Garden', *Landscape Architecture*, November 1979, pp. 610–613.

Keen, Mary, 'Landscape of Neglect', *Independent on Sunday*, 15 April 1990, p. 55.

Lancaster, Michael, 'Roberto Burle Marx', *Hortus*, 2 Summer 1987, pp. 42–48.

'The Lightning Field', *Art Journal*, Fall 1982.

Barragán, Luis, 'Mexico', *Landscape Architecture*, January 1982, pp. 68ff.

Macay, David, *Architectural Review*, 85, vol. 9, pp. 60–67.

Marx, Roberto Burle, *Garden Design*, Spring 83, 26, 31.

_____*Landscape Architecture*, May 1981.

Neall, Lynne Creighton (ed), *Lawrence Halprin: changing places*, San Francisco Museum of Modern Art, San Francisco, 1986.

Riley, Robert B., 'On the Perils of Meaning', *Places*, vol. 3, no. 3.

Small, Glen, 'The Green Machine', *Landscape Architecture*, September 1979, p. 482.

Smithson, Robert, *Landscape Architecture*, January/February 1985, p. 94.

_____*Process Architecture*, 1985, August, no. 61, pp. 1–151.

SEATTLE FREEWAY PARK

'Park atop a Freeway', *AIA Journal*, June 1983, pp. 43–47.

HARLEQUIN PLAZA

Goldstein, Barbara, 'Harlequin Plaza', *Landscape Architecture*, July/August 1979, pp. 56–59.

JARDINS DE TURIA

Peter Hodgkinson, 'Gardens in Spain', *Progressive Architecture*, June 1984, pp. 89–92.

LONGFELLOW GARDEN

'Longfellow Garden', *Landscape Architecture*, September/October 1985, pp. 69–71.

PARQUE TEZOZOMOC

Schjetnan, Mario, 'Myth, History and Culture', *Landscape Architecture*, March/April 1984, pp. 75–9.

SAN JOSE PLAZA PARK

Progressive Architecture, July 1986, p. 70.

SUTTON PLACE

Architect's Journal, November 19, 1986, pp. 67–70.

Landscape Design, October 1983.

Spens, Michael, 'Admirable Jellicoe', *Architectural Review*, September 1989, pp. 85–92.

Studio International, Vol. 196, p. 999, 1983.

PARC DE LA CORDERIE ROYALE

Burkhardt, Lucius, and Donadieu, Pierre, 'La Démarche Paysagère de Bernard Lassus', *Paysage & Amenagement*, No. 3, May 1985, pp. 17–41.

Jacobs, Peter, and Poullaouec-Gonidec, Philippe, 'Red Dots and other Tales', *Landscape Architecture*, January 1989.

Journal of Garden History, April/June 1983, pp. 79–107.

J. PAUL GETTY MUSEUM

Gebhard, David, *Architecture Plus*, vol. 2, no. 5, September/October 1974, pp. 56–61.

RIO SHOPPING CENTER

'New American Landscape', *Progressive Architecture*, July 1989.

PARQUE DEL CLOT

Buchanan, Peter, 'Barcelona park & plaza', *Architectural Review*, September 1989, pp. 81–84.

FOUNTAIN PLAZA

Landscape Architecture, 1986, pp. 50–57.

Price, Martin, 'Dallas Oasis', *Places*, vol. 4, no. 4, pp. 33–35.

PARC DE LA VILLETTE

Buchanan, Peter, 'La Villette Park', *Architectural Review*, September 1985, pp. 72–74.

Landscape Architecture, 1983, July/August, pp. 66 ff.

Landscape Architecture (UK), March 1988, pp. 30 ff.

BAMBOO GARDEN, PARC DE LA VILLETTE

Casabella, 47, June 1983, pp. 12–23.

STOCKLEY PARK

Davey, Peter, 'Stockley Park', *Architectural Review*, September 1989, pp. 42–48.

ROBSON SQUARE
Erickson, Arthur, *The Architecture of Arthur Erickson*,
Vancouver, 1988.
Landscape Architecture, May 1979; *Landscape Architecture*,
July 1979, p. 377.
Nairn, Janet, 'Vancouver's Grand New Government
Centre', *Architectural Record*, December 1980, pp.
65–75.

WINTER GARDEN, Niagara Falls
Stephens, Suzanne, 'Niagara Rises', *Progressive
Architecture*, August 1978.

TSUKUBA CIVIC CENTRE
Landscape Architecture, July/August 1985, pp. 71–77.

BRION CEMETERY
Scarpa, Carlo, 'Brion cemetery, S. Vito', *Architectural
Review*, September 1985.

EMILIO'S FOLLY
Landscape Architecture, January 1982, pp. 68–75.

LITTLE SPARTA
Bann, Stephen, 'A Description of Stonypath', *Journal of
Landscape History*, Vol. 1, No. 2, pp. 113–144.
Burkhardt, Lucius, 'Ian Hamilton Finlay's Expressive
Garden', *Anthos*, 4, 1984, pp. 2–8.

AICHI GREEN CENTRE
Landscape Architecture, 1980, pp. 481–514.
Marx, Doug, 'Zen and the art of landscape design',
Northwest, 15 October 1989, pp. 10–14.
Murase, Robert, 'The Language of Stone', *Landscape
Architecture*, November 1979, pp. 589–92.

CALIFORNIA SCENARIO
Goldstein, Barbara, 'California Scenario', *Arts and
Architecture*, vol. 1, no. 4 pp. 16–21.
Landscape Architecture, January/February 1985, pp. 58ff.
Tomlinson, David, in *Landscape Architecture*, May 1982,
pp. 56–57.

EUDOXIA
Boles, Daralice D., in *Progressive Architecture*, July 1989,
pp. 53–55.
Johnson, Jory, 'Michael Van Valkenburgh', *Progressive
Architecture*, July 1989, pp. 70–77.
Van Valkenburgh, Michael R., 'Eudoxia: A new civic
landscape', *Places*, vol. 3, no. 3, pp. 18–19.

TERRAIN, O'Hare International Center
Feinberg, Jean E., 'Terrain', *Landscape Architecture*, May/
June 1987, p. 82.
Landscape Architecture, March 1988.
Sasaki, Yoji, 'Elyn Zimmerman', *Japan Landscape*, No.
11, 1989, pp. 98–101.
Zimmer, William, *New York Times*, 10 July 1988, p. 24.

BASE DE PLEIN AIR ET LOISIRS, Cergy Neuville
Cavilie, Bernard, 'Innovative Design at Cergy New
Town', *Landscape Architecture*, January 1978, pp.
38–42.

GAS WORKS PARK
Hester, Randolf T., 'Process can be Style', *Landscape
Architecture*, May/June 1983.
Thompson, J. William, 'Landscape of Dream, Warrior
of Vision', *Art on File*, September 1989, pp. 81–87.
'Richard Haag Associates, Gas Works Park, Seattle,
Washington', *Landscape Architecture*, September 1989,
pp. 81 ff.
Weems, Sally, 'Gas Works Park', *Landscape Australia*, 1/
80, 1980, pp. 23–30.

SOLANA
Barna, Joel W., 'Solana in the Sun', *Progressive
Architecture*, April 1989, pp. 65–74.
'IBM Westlake/Southlake', *Southern Landscape
Architecture*, September/October 1989, pp. 15–20.
Jarmusch, Ann, 'Solana', *Landscape Architecture*, October
1985, pp 72–75.
Sasaki, Yoji (ed), 'Peter Walker: landscape as art', *Process
Architecture*, 85, October 1989, complete issue.
Process Architecture, March 1988, p. 111.

PHOTO CREDITS

ACKNOWLEDGMENTS

The author and publishers wish to thank the following for supplying photographs. Where no credit is indicated the illustrations have been supplied by the relevant designer or the design practice.

Glen Allen/SWA: p. 49; Architectural Association/Gerald Davies: p. 15; Arup Associates: pp. 124, 125 (*b*), 126 (*bl*), 126/7, 126 (*br*), 127 (*b*); Hélène Binet: pp. 164(*t*), 164 (*b*), 165, 168, 169; Ricardo Bofill: pp. 50/51, 51 (*b*), 52, 53; Crispin Boyle/Arup Associates: p. 125 (*t*); Raoul Bunschoten: pp. 166(*t*), 166 (*b*), 167; Bureau de Paysages, Paris: p. 118(*b*); Jim Burns: p. 35; Stefan Buzas: pp. 154–9 inclusive; Gerry Campbell/SWA: pp. 26/7, 46/7; Dixi Carrillo/SWA: pp. 46 (*l*), 47 (*t*); CB Foto, Barcelona: p. 104 (*b*); Louis Checkman: pp. 170/71 inclusive; Harry Cobb: p. 109 (*t*); Country Life: pp. 16 (*tr*), 16 (*cr*); John Donat: p. 192/3; Garden and Landscape Pictures: pp. 70/71, 71 (*t*), 71 (*b*), 74 (*l*), 74/5; Alastair Gordon: p. 214/15; Richard Haag: pp. 205–7 inclusive; Lawrence Halprin: pp. 13 (*t*), 37 (*t*), 37 (*b*); Hargreaves Associates: pp. 64–7 inclusive; Bryan Hunt: p. 106; Yasuhiro Ishimoto: pp. 149 (*t*), 150/51, 151 (*r*), 232/3; Preben Jakobsen: pp. 198/9, 208, 209, 210, 210/11; Sir Geoffrey Jellicoe: pp. 10, 11 (*l*), 11 (*r*), 12 (*l*), 68 (*t*), 68 (*b*); Aaron Kiley: p. 113 (*r*); Office of Dan Kiley: pp. 108 (*t*), 109 (*b*), 110/11, 112/13; KLM: p. 19; Atelier Bernard Lassus/Monika Nikolic: p. 82 (*b*); E. Lennard: p. 98/9; Andrew Mahaddie: pp. 194, 195; Michael McQueen: p. 173(*t*); Tim McAllister: p. 204; Mike McKee: pp. 218, 225; Satoru Mishima: p. 149 (*b*); Dee Mullen: p. 34; National Trust/John Bethell: pp. 84, 85; National Trust/Tony Cook: pp. 86 (*t*), 86 (*b*), 86/7; Niagara Falls Chamber of Commerce: p. 142 (*tl*); PWMS C. Rion: p. 102; Antonia Reeve: p. 172 (*t*); Rizzo/Creative: p. 103 (*t*); Julius Shulman: pp. 28 (*t*), 93, 94, 94/5, 96, 97; Julius Shulman/Carlos von Frankenberg: p. 29; Ellen Soe/Clifton Design: pp. 147 (*t*), 147(*b*); Sources/Atlanta: p. 103 (*b*); Morley von Sternberg: pp. 38–43 inclusive; SWA Group: p. 44; Daniel D. Stewart: pp. 212/13, 213, 216 (*l*); Jessica Strang (courtesy of Copijn Utrecht Groenadviseurs): pp. 128–131 inclusive; Tim Street-Porter: pp. 162/3, 185 (*t*), 185 (*b*), 186, 187, 188/9, 189 (*r*); H. Thanhauser: p. 136/7; Frank J. Thomas: p. 12 (*r*); C. W. Thomsen: p. 138(*tl*); Margaret Turner: pp. 69, 73; David Walker: pp. 219, 220 (*t*), 220 (*b*), 222, 223 (*t*), 223 (*b*), 224; Office of Peter Walker/Martha Schwartz: pp. 101 (*t*), 101 (*b*); Dai Williams: p. 36; Elyn Zimmerman: pp. 196 (*t*), 197 (*b*).

I have to acknowledge the great help of a number of people: Val Riches, who worked as my research assistant; Elisabeth Ingles, who moulded the raw manuscript, and who is the only editor with whom I have ever remained on good terms; Stefan Buzas, who guided me through Scarpa's Brion cemetery and provided the photographs; the staffs of the libraries of the Royal Institute of British Architects and the Landscape Institute, who were helpful far beyond the call of duty. Special thanks go to Shelley Power, Tim Street-Porter, the wonderful Sir Geoffrey Jellicoe and the designers of the projects and their staffs, who have been universally kind. They include Yoshiko Amiya of Arata Isozaki Associates, Cathy Blake at Peter Walker and Partners, Collette Berthier at Alexandre Chemetoff, Noel Best at Arthur Erickson, Alexandre Chemetoff, J'ørn Copijn, Philip Cave, Valeri Clarke at Lawrence Halprin, William Callaway of SWA Group, Fabienne Ducellier of Bernard Lassus, Kathryn Drinkhouse of Martha Schwartz, Roger DeWeese, Arthur Erickson, Allen Fong, Dani Freixes, Ian Hamilton Finlay, M. Paul Friedberg, Barbara Goldstein, George Hargreaves, John Hopkins, Lawrence Halprin, Peter Hodgkinson, Richard Haag, Robert Holden, Arata Isozaki, Preben Jakobsen, Dan Kiley, Denis Kurutz, Bernard Lassus, Hans Lutz, Laura Laterman at Ricardo Bofill's Taller de Arquitectura, Andrew Mahaddie, David Meyer, Dee Mullin at Lawrence Halprin, Eric J. Mullendore at Michael Van Valkenburgh Associates, Mercedes at Dani Freixes, Michele Massot at API, Robert Murase, Vicente Miranda, Neil Porter, Richard Pete at Dan Kiley, Peter Rawstorne, Daniel D. Stewart, Ken Smith, Lori Starr at the J. Paul Getty Museum, Mario Schjetnan, Martha Schwartz, Richard Sullivan of Weintraub & di Domenico, Bernard Tschumi, Margaret Turner, Tom Turner, Michael Van Valkenburgh, Michel Viollet, Emmet L. Wemple, James Wines, Lee Weintraub, Peter Walker, Ruth Webber, Anna Ydarra at Peter Walker & Partners, Elyn Zimmerman.

INDEX